A GUIDE TO PHOTOGRAPHY

by

CHARLES SWEDLUND

1967

770
S

the PHOTOGRAPHER, dependent upon his
environment, ventures into the world
seeking images.

the PHOTOGRAPHER is forced to look
beyond the superficial. a PHOTOGRAPH
should be a new experience.

the PHOTOGRAPH, as a factual record,
is an effective medium for the inter-
change of ideas.

the PHOTOGRAPH enables the photographer
to present visually his feelings and
ideas.

ACKNOWLEDGMENTS

I would like to thank the following
people who helped me prepare this
book: Oscar Bailey, Paul Bryant,
Jean Delius, Margie and Darryl
Hughto, Elise Kling, Elinor Ward,
and Lorraine Whyer.

C O N T E N T S

PHOTOGRAPHY - A BRIEF HISTORY

The word "photography" comes from the Greek words meaning "light" and "writing." Light is the basic ingredient of all photography and is used by the camera to form an image optically. In printing, light was again used in conjunction with certain chemicals to secure the resulting image. Each of these two scientific curiosities was known separately for many years, but they were not used together to make a photographic print until 1837.

Early photographers used materials which were radically different from those used today. Their efforts, however, form the foundation for present day techniques. The influence of these techniques on the imagery of the photographs will not be considered here. This broad and complicated subject is best handled in a book dedicated to that purpose. The following briefly traces the evolution of photographic materials.

CAMERA OBSCURA

The camera obscura, as it was originally called, was a light tight box with a lens at one end and a piece of frosted glass at the other. The lens of the camera obscura gathered light which was reflected from a scene and produced an image of the scene on the ground glass. The image was in perfect proportion and perspective. A sheet of translucent paper could be laid on the ground glass and the scene could be traced. This was an answer to a problem which had troubled everyone who had attempted to draw a scene "realistically." It served as a means of copying nature without the skill and knowledge of a draftsman. Leonardo da Vinci, for example, used the camera obscura in drawing his sketches. As years passed, many variations of the apparatus were devised. One of the most elaborate was a camera obscura large enough to accomodate a person. A person who stood inside was able to trace the image on a translucent paper inside the camera. Other variations were less cumbersome and could be readily carried from place to place. Many camera obscuras became toys in wealthy households.

Camera Obscuras

2

HEINRICH SCHULZE (1727)

Certain materials, particularly silver salts, were found to be
sensitive to light. These chemicals, it was found, turned black
when exposed to light. Heating the chemicals had no effect upon
them. A German chemist, *Heinrich Schulze*, first noticed this and
began conducting experiments. He cut a stencil of opaque paper,
wrapped it around a transparent jar of chemicals and placed the jar
in bright sunlight. Upon exposure to the sunlight, only the exposed areas turned black. The unexposed portions remained white,
but eventually turned black as Schulze admired his discovery.

THOMAS WEDGWOOD (1802)

Another person, *Thomas Wedgwood*, the son of the British potter,
pursued the same type of experiments by soaking paper in light-
sensitive chemicals. When he laid lace on the paper, the exposed
portions turned black, while the unexposed portions remained white.
Because he was not able to make the images permanent, his experiments were also futile. Ill health ended the continuation of his
experiments. Wedgwood, however, was on the right path, for his
two basic practices later proved to be useful. The first practice
involved the negative-positive relationship. The opaque lace per-
mitted no light to pass through it. The portion of the paper covered by the lace remained white, while the exposed areas turned
black. This produced an image which was a reversal in tone of the
lace, essentially a negative. The second practice included the use
of the camera obscura. Wedgwood's experiments failed however, because of the slow reaction of the light sensitive materials to sunlight.

JOSEPH NICEPHORE NIEPCE (1826)

Joseph Nicephore Niepce, a French inventor, succeeded where Schulze
and Wedgwood failed. He succeeded in making his images permanent
and became the first photographer. His success stemmed from the
experiments he conducted involving lithography. He discovered that
certain chemicals, for example those found in varnish, became insol-
uble upon exposure to light. A thin tin plate, coated with this
light-sensitive varnish, was exposed in the camera obscura. Placing
the exposed plate in a weak acid allowed the areas on the plate
which had not been exposed to light to be etched. This plate, upon
being incised deeper by hand, was inked and printed. This process
offered the first Photo-Mechanical reproduction. Ill health and lack
of money led Niepce to enter a partnership with Louis Daguerre.

LOUIS JACQUES MANDE DAGUERRE (Daguerrotype - 1839)

Louis Jacques Mande Daguerre was a wealthy painter and the inventor of the *Diorama*. The Diorama consisted of large realistic paintings which were illuminated from behind. They were transparencies. With a system of shutters and screens, the mood of a painting was changed by allowing light to emphasize one area and then another. Because of his concern for realism, Daguerre began to experiment with a camera obscura and light sensitive materials. He became aware that another gentleman, Niepce, was conducting similar experiments. Finally, after correspondance and some mutual distrust, they formed a partnership. The partnership was short lived due to Niepce's death. Daguerre continued to experiment for eleven years. Finally, in 1839, using chemicals which Niepce never tried, Daguerre was able to make photography practical.

Niepce Invented Photography and Daguerre Made It Practical.

Daguerre, feeling that he had changed the process sufficiently, called his efforts *daguerrotypes*. Upon revealing his process, Daguerre became world famous.

A daguerrotype was made from a sheet of copper with one side silverplated. This surface was buffed until it looked like a mirror, was subjected to certain chemicals which made the plate light sensitive, and then, was exposed in a camera. After exposure, the plate was developed with fumes from boiling mercury, thus producing a visible image. The permanance of this image was secured by soaking the plate in hypo and then rinsing with water.

A daguerrotype was rather difficult to look at because of its mirror-like surface. From certain angles, the image appeared as a negative. The viewer also saw his own reflection. The surface of a daguerrotype was very delicate and was therefore covered with glass and a brass frame which were placed in an ornate, protective case.

The exposure of daguerrotypes was rather long (20 - 40 seconds). Young children, because of their difficulty in remaining still, were hard to photograph. Neck clamps were used in order that the subject could lean back, thus making movement less likely.

Each daguerrotype was unique. The material exposed in the camera became the finished photograph. Duplication was difficult due to the mirror-like surface, yet the demand for daguerrotype portraits was great even though they were not cheap. The daguerrotype reigned for about fifteen years, but was finally replaced by less complicated and more economical processes.

FOX TALBOT   (Talbotype - 1835)

While Niepce and Daguerre were conducting their experiments, an
English scientist, *Fox Talbot*, was doing similar work. He was
not aware of the experiments of Niepce and Daguerre. On hearing
of Daguerre's success, Talbot made his bid for fame. His experiments consisted of using paper which was made light sensitive. He
rediscovered the idea of the negative-positive relationship. He
then realized that from a paper negative any number of positive
prints may be made. Since the daguerrotype lacked this ease of
duplication, the use of a negative was desirable. However, the
quality of the *talbotypes* left much to be desired. Because of
the necessary exposure through the paper negative, much detail and texture was lost. Talbotypes had a soft, unsharp quality and lacked the
public appeal of the sharply defined daguerrotype.

Both daguerrotypes and talbotypes presented problems because neither
process possessed both of the desirable qualities, qualitative imagery and ease of duplication. In hoping to solve this problem,
glass seemed to be the answer. Glass, lacking the coarseness of
paper, allowed for sharp imagery and easy duplication. Many agreed
that glass was the answer, but it was still a problem since glass
was a very difficult material on which to adhere anything. Many
techniques and materials were tried. One man even tried the slime
from snails. A compound containing egg white was partially successful.

SCOTT ARCHER   (Collodian-Wet Plate - 1851)

An English sculptor, *Scott Archer*, devised a method called *collodian*,
which proved most successful. The *collodian* or *wet plate process*
consisted of coating a piece of glass with a film of collodian, a
chemical compound which, upon drying, forms a skin-like film which
adheres to glass, forming an emulsion. The coated glass plate was
emersed in light sensitive chemicals and, while wet, it was exposed
in the camera. The plate then had to be developed immediately because as the chemicals dried they lost their light sensitive properties.

AMBROTYPE   (1850's)

The *ambrotype*, a variation of the collodian process, became very
popular in the United States because of the great demand for inexpensive portraiture. The ambrotype consisted of a piece of glass
coated with a collodian emulsion, purposely underexposed. As a
result of this underexposure an image was very pale. This pale
image, when viewed against white, had the appearance of an underexposed negative. When viewed against black, the image appeared
to be a properly exposed positive. These photographs were also

encased in pressed paper or leather cases in the same manner as the daguerrotypes. The ambrotype was easier to produce and less expensive than the daguerrotype and eventually replaced it.

TINTYPE (1870's)

The *tintype*, another variation of the collodian process was also extremely popular during the latter part of the 1800's. It differed from the ambrotype in that a sheet of tin was used instead of a sheet of glass. Again, collodian was applied to the sheet of tin. Because of the black undercoat provided by the tin, a tintype never had the brilliance which a daguerrotype or an ambrotype had. It lacked a pure white. It was, however, the least expensive of the three and became the product of the "cheaper" portrait photographers.

Daguerrotype

Ambrotype

Tintype

CARTE-DE-VISITE (1860's)

The third variation of the collodian process was the *carte-de-visite*. It retained the basic idea of the collodian process by producing a negative on a piece of glass from which prints might be made. However, because the cameras used multiple lenses, a number of exposures, usually from six to eight, were produced on one negative. The resulting negative would then be contact printed, and the photographs mounted individually on 4" x 2 1/2" cards. The carte-de-visite eliminated the two major handicaps of the previous processes described, that of being limited by only one final photograph and that of cost.

6

Additional copies could be made at any time from the negative. As a
result, the carte-de-visite became very popular and was used for a
long period of time.

Other photographers who were not involved in commercial portraiture
were also using the collodian process to produce printable negatives.
Their glass negatives, after being processed and dried, were brought
back to a permanent darkroom. There the negatives were contact printed
on light sensitive paper and when processed, produced positive prints.
The size of a photographic print depended on the size of the negative.
For example, an 8" x 10" photograph was only made from an 8" x 10"
negative. Enlarging, as practiced today, was not then possible. As
a result, the cameras used were quite large. Early photographs display
the fortitude of these pioneer photographers. Their equipment included
heavy, cumbersome cameras as well as processing materials. Bisson
Freres combated the cold of the Swiss mountains, Vroman worked in the
heat of the desert. Brady photographed the ravages of the Civil War.
The collodian process, which replaced previous processes, prospered
for over thirty years.

THE DRY PLATE

The daguerrotype, collodian, ambrotype, tintype and carte-de-visite
processes all required that the photographer have a darkroom where-
ever he photographed. Plates which were used had to be sensitized
and processed on location.

As technology improved, the *dry plate* came into existence. It consisted
of a glass plate which was coated with gelatin containing light sensitive chemicals which could be exposed in a dry state. Dry plates, which
could be purchased in stores, enabled the photographer to buy his
plates, photograph at his leisure, and process his plates any time
thereafter.

ROLL FILM

George Eastman, a small manufacturer of dry plates who lived in Rochester,
New York, sought to reduce the weight clumsiness and fragile nature of
the glass plate. He devised a method by which the emulsion could be
applied to a flexible support. At first he used paper, but later substituted nitro-cellulose. This new material, while possessing all the
qualities of glass, had the advantage of being light in weight and flexible. The flexible nature of the transparent plastic allowed the film
to be rolled. To accommodate the roll film, Eastman made a camera in
the shape of a small easily held box - the first *box camera*. In this box
camera there was enough film for one hundred photographs. The film,

after being exposed, was sent to Rochester while still in the camera. There it was processed, printed and returned by mail.

The introduction of roll film began a new system in photography. It enabled the mechanics of camera operation to be simplified and brought about the use of the small, hand-held camera.

COLOR PHOTOGRAPHY

The desire for color was apparent from the beginning and many techniques and ideas were attempted. The majority of the processes were very complicated and resulted in poor renditions of the original subject. With present day processes and materials the techniques are simplified and the colors more faithfully reproduced.

POLAROID PHOTOGRAPHY (1947)

In 1947 *Edwin H. Land* introduced *Polaroid* film materials consisting at first only of black and white and now including color. The Polaroid process eliminated a problem that has always plagued photographers, the delay in time between exposure and examination of the finished photograph. The Polaroid film contains the necessary chemicals in pods which are released and spread as the film is drawn between rollers in the camera. As a result, the image is both developed and fixed while still in the camera and after ten or sixty seconds a finished photograph is ready. The disadvantage of this is that there is generally no usable negative which makes duplication and enlargements inconvenient. In order to make duplications and enlargements the original print must be photographed which is expensive and results in loss of quality.

The materials photographers have used have changed drastically in the short period of time photography has been possible. With new technological developments such as Xerox, the Laser and Video tape, the history of photography is actually only at its beginning.

CAMERAS

The question "Which camera is best for me?" is a hard one to answer.
The variety of cameras on the market is confusing. It is important
to consider one's particular need and to avoid being a victim of old
cliches and advertising. It is also important not to use equipment
which requires knowledge and skill beyond one's ability. A camera,
as any tool, must be understood in order to be used successfully. One
camera is not versatile enough for every need. As a result, one must
make a careful choice. Possible choices include the following:

1. Sub-Miniature Cameras
2. 35 mm Cameras
3. Roll Film Cameras
4. Press Cameras
5. View Cameras

Within these catagories, cameras are described in accordance with the
methods they use for focusing.

1. SUB-MINIATURE CAMERAS

Many small sub-miniature cameras (spy cameras) appeared from time to
time, but were usually of poor quality. They were toys or novelties.
World War II changed this. The Germans and the Japanese developed
highly effective sub-miniature cameras for espionage. After the war,
many of these were sold on the market. Other companies began to market their own versions. Today there is a wide variety from which to
choose. People desire the sub-miniature camera because these cameras
are even easier to carry than a small 35 mm camera. One sub-miniature
camera, the Minox, is the same size as a pack of gum, and is easily
carried in a pocket. The developing and printing is done by a specialized
lab because of the necessary care and specialized equipment needed to process and print the small film. The subminiature camera, therefore, is not
recommended for general use.

2. 35 mm CAMERAS

The first 35 mm cameras were made to use 35 mm motion picture film,
in order to photograph movie sets for lighting tests. Photographers
began purchasing these small cameras, which encouraged manufacturers
to market them. The 35 mm camera is now popular throughout the world.
There are three methods of focusing 35 mm cameras.

One method of focusing with an inexpensive 35 mm camera is by *estimating the distance* between the subject and the camera and making the proper adjustments. The distance to the subject can be estimated by observing how large a person is in the view finder. A camera must be about ten feet away from a person standing, in order to photograph him (A).

A   B   C

If a person is half as small as the area in the viewfinder (B), the person is roughly twenty feet away from the camera. If only half of the person is included in the viewfinder (C), the person is roughly five feet from the camera.

These inexpensive cameras are slightly more expensive than the non-adjustable (box) cameras, but not as expensive as cameras with the rangefinder or ground glass method of focusing.

The second method of focusing makes use of a *rangefinder*. A rangefinder is a mechanical device which produces two images in the camera's viewfinder. One image is usually tinted light green or red for better visibility. As the lens is moved in and out, usually by rotation, the two images coincide. The camera is then focused on that particular object. See the following illustration.

Split image rangefinder   Coincidental rangefinder

A rangefinder is accurate up to three feet from the subject. The price range for a 35 mm rangefinder type of camera is approximately $35 to $400. Many inexpensive models are imported from Japan and some are of good quality. Some 35 mm rangefinder cameras allow for interchangeable lenses (medium to expensive versions), permitting the use of wide angle and telephoto lenses. The rangefinder type of camera is cheaper to construct and as a result, is lower in price than the single lens reflex camera. For some photographers, for example, the journalistic photographer, the rangefinder type of camera has decisive advantages over the single lens reflex camera.

The rangefinder type of camera is quieter in operation because of fewer moving parts. Some people feel that it also has the advantage of being faster in operation, particularly in focusing. The rangefinder type of 35 mm camera is the most popular, and offers the widest selection.

The third method of focusing is used by the more expensive *single lens reflex* cameras. These allow one to view the subject directly through the camera lens, rotating it to focus on the desired subject. The photographer is able to visualize exactly what the composition will be. Rangefinder cameras have charts and scales indicating, in feet, what is in focus and what is out of focus. However, these indications are not visual, and it is impossible to tell what the out of focus areas will look like by reading a chart. Focusing is visual and natural with the single lens reflex, and one of the thrills of using it is the moment the image comes into focus. The price of the cheapest single lens reflex camera begins at about $150, considerably more than the cheapest rangefinder camera. The single lens reflex camera usually has provisions for interchangeable lenses. See the diagram on page 14, illustrating the single lens reflex camera.

Because one may actually look through the camera lens, the single lens reflex is ideal for close-ups and extreme telephoto situations. There is no problem of *parallax*. Parallax refers to the difference between the image seen through the view finder and that which is recorded by the film. This is due to the different positions of the view finder and the camera lens.

Photography situations which demand the use of an extreme telephoto lens are not possible with rangefinder cameras, as the rangefinders are not accurate enough. With accessories, a few rangefinder cameras convert to single lens reflex cameras, but this practice is expensive and awkward.

The single lens reflex camera is somewhat noisy in operation which is a consideration in some situations. The first models were quite troublesome and slow in operation because they had more manual adjustments than a rangefinder camera. Advancements in design have now eliminated these difficulties. The present single lens reflex camera is an ideal camera for anyone who can afford a moderately priced 35 mm camera.

The small compact nature of the 35 mm camera appealed to the journalist and the traveler, but the use of color brought it to the Sunday photographers. The 35 mm color slide is the cheapest and easiest method of enjoying color. If color slides are the desired end result of one's photography, the 35 mm camera is an ideal choice.

3. ROLL FILM CAMERAS

Roll film cameras are the largest group of cameras available. The
rapid growth of this type of camera produced a vast number of cameras varying in size, type and quality. Many of these cameras have
only slight differences. However, some classifications may be made.
by considering the different methods of focusing which are used.

        A. Non-adjustable (box camera)
        B. Estimating the distance
        C. Rangefinder
        D. Single lens reflex
        E. Twin lens reflex

The first roll film camera was the box camera, introduced in 1889
by George Eastman. With its ease of operation and economy, this
type of camera introduced photography to the general public. The
box camera then rapidly became a household item. With economy as
the primary concern, it was not a very versatile camera. It was
simply made to be used on bright, sunny days and was the Sunday
afternoon camera.

The box camera was the first of the *non-adjustable* cameras. The
non-adjustable camera, although a compromise between quality and
economy, is a serious and satisfactory camera as long as one recog-
nizes and respects its limitations. Focusing, aperture and shutter
speed are set during manufacture. The F/Number of these cameras is
usually set at F/16 which provides adequate depth of field and eliminates focusing. As long as the subject is six feet from the camera,
relative sharpness may be obtained. An aperture of F/16 requires a
bright, sunny day and as long as that is respected, correct exposures
are possible. Attempting to use this type of camera on a dull,
cloudy day produces negatives too underexposed to yield satisfactory
photographs. The shutter speed on an old non-adjustable (box) camera was approximately 1/30 of a second, which presented problems. It
is extremely difficult to hand hold a camera or stop action at that
slow shutter speed. The present non-adjustable cameras, for example,
Instamatics (Kodak) have a 1/90 of a second shutter speed which helps
to eliminate this problem.

That the non-adjustable camera requires the subject to be at least
six feet distant is a limitation. However, supplementary lenses
may be attached, allowing photographs to be taken with the subject
at a distance of three feet from the camera. These lenses are called portrait lenses and are quite inexpensive. Care is needed when
looking through the camera's viewfinder at close subjects. The
viewfinder does not accurately show what the camera photographs.
This discrepancy is called parallax. It is important to remove the
portrait lens when photographing objects far away. Otherwise, the
resulting photographs are out of focus.

The *folding-out camera* became popular as an improvement over the original box camera and was, for a time, the dominant type of roll film camera. It required an estimation of the distance from the subject to the camera. Folding-out cameras varied in size and quality. Some made use of rather large film which is now difficult to obtain. The front of this type of camera had a scale which had to be adjusted in order to focus on subjects at different distances. The shutter speed was also adjustable, providing the camera with a fair amount of versatility.

Only a few roll film cameras make use of the rangefinder method of focusing. The method of operation is similar to that of the 35 mm camera discussed on page 9 .

There are only three main roll film cameras which are single lens reflexes. These are the Hasselblad (Swedish), the Bronica (Japanese), and the Rolleiflex (German). Each of these cameras is rather expensive. Basically, they are similar in operation to the 35 mm single lens reflex camera. The main exception includes a separate and removable magazine system for the film. The magazine may be removed with a partially exposed roll of film in it without endangering the film and may be replaced at a later time and the remainder of the film roll exposed. This is especially useful in using black and white and color film in the same camera. A diagram illustrating the roll film single lens reflex camera is on pages 14 and 15.

The *twin lens reflex* method of focusing is unique to the roll film camera. It has two lenses, one for focusing and the other for exposing the film. The two lenses are mounted in such a manner as to enable a person to move them back and forth together. As the image on the ground glass is focused, the lens for exposing the film is simultaneously focused. See the diagram on page 14 illustrating the twin lens reflex camera.

Because the size of the negative allows for quality enlargements, the twin lens reflex is a wise choice if black and white photographs are desired. Color film for the twin lens reflex camera is considerably more expensive than that for the 35 mm camera. The twin lens reflex camera is the best compromise between the large view camera and the small 35 mm camera. It is light, easy to operate, and uses readily available film.

4. PRESS CAMERA

The press camera is a 4" x 5" semi-portable view camera which
newspaper photographers have used. The press cameras are rapidly being replaced by the twin lens reflexes and the 35 mm cameras.
For interior exposures press cameras require flash bulbs or strobe-
electronic flash which produces harshly lit subjects that may look
somewhat unnatural.

5. VIEW CAMERA

The view camera was the earliest camera made, and differs very
little, even today, from the camera obscura. It is a large camera which uses film in sheet form. The film is loaded into holders, each with provision for two sheets of film. Common film
sizes are 4" x 5", 5" x 7", and 8" x 10". An 8" x 10" print,
contact printed from an 8" x 10" negative, produces the ultimate
in quality because no quality is lost in enlargement. Focusing
with a view camera is accomplished by looking at the ground glass.
A black cloth is used to shield extraneous light in order for one
to see the ground glass image. The view camera has adjustments
which the miniature cameras lack. These adjustments enable the
photographer to control perspective and depth of field. This
feature makes the view camera important for many commercial
applications. See the diagram of the view camera on page 14.

BASIC CAMERA ACCESSORIES

After having chosen a camera, the photographer needs four basic
accessories in order that he may obtain its maximum versatility.
One is the *cable release*, a flexible shaft which enables the shutter to be tripped without moving the camera. This is especially
useful when using slow shutter speeds. Another is an *exposure
meter* which gives a quick and accurate means of determining exposures. A third accessory, the *lens shade*, helps to keep extraneous light rays from entering the camera through the lens. The
fourth necessity is a *tripod*, a three-legged support for holding
the camera steady at a given, fixed position.

FOUR BASIC METHODS OF FOCUSING

Rangefinder

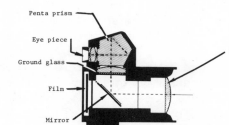

Single Lens Reflex

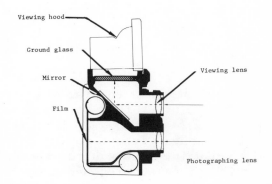

Twin Lens Reflex

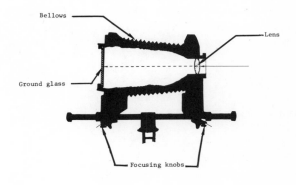

Ground Glass

VERSATILITY OF A CAMERA

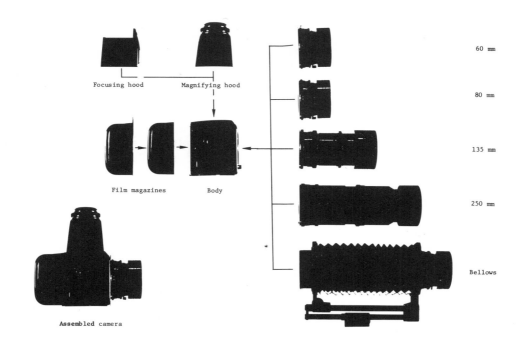

Focusing hood   Magnifying hood

Film magazines   Body

60 mm

80 mm

135 mm

250 mm

Bellows

Assembled camera

RANGEFINDER CAMERA COMPARED TO THE SINGLE LENS REFLEX

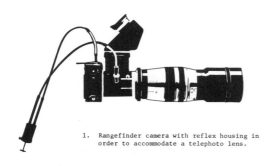

1. Rangefinder camera with reflex housing in order to accommodate a telephoto lens.

3. Single lens reflex camera with a telephoto lens.

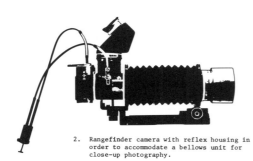

2. Rangefinder camera with reflex housing in order to accommodate a bellows unit for close-up photography.

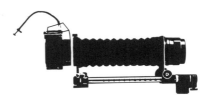

4. Single lens reflex camera with a bellows unit for close-up photography.

EXPOSURE

The exposure meter is a valuable aid to the photographer. It allows
for an accurate and consistent manner of determining exposures. An
exposure meter is an integral part of the necessary photographic
equipment. It is a device which contains cells which produce small
amounts of electricity when exposed to light. This electricity is
coupled with an armature which rotates, moving a lever or pointer.
The pointer moves on a calibrated scale which, in turn, is translated
into F/Number and shutter speed combinations. The scale on the exposure meter allows one to decide which F/Number and shutter speed may
be used for correct exposure. The scale also indicates which F/Number
and shutter speed combination will stop the fastest action and produce the greatest amount of depth of field for that particular situation. There are two different types of exposure meters:

> 1. The Reflected Light Meter
> 2. The Incident Light Meter

1. THE REFLECTED LIGHT METER

As seen in the following diagram, the reflected light meter measures
light which is reflected from a subject. As the meter is pointed
towards different objects in a subject the needle fluctuates. A light
object produces a high reading, and conversely, a dark object produces
a low reading. After observing the range of readings, an average is
generally used in determining the exposure.

The bright side of the barn and the sky in the above illustration produce high meter readings; the grass produces an average reading. The
shadow portion of the barn and the roof produce low readings. The
correct exposure can be determined by averaging the five readings.

The booklet or instruction manual which accompanies the meter should be
read carefully. Although all reflected light meters are similar, the
manners of operation vary from one manufacturer to another. A complete
familiarization with the meter is essential.

The manner in which readings are obtained is important. If readings are taken incorrectly, the resulting exposures may be either excessive or insufficient. There are four common mistakes made in reading reflected light meters. The meter may be held too far from the subject or pointed too high. In both cases the reading taken may be from the sky and the subject will be underexposed. On the other hand, the meter may be held so close to the subject that it is reading its own shadow, or it may be aimed too low and include only the foreground. In these cases, the subject would be overexposed. The correct method involves pointing the meter slightly downward, taking an average reading of the sky and the foreground.

A subject, for this example a person, which is lit from behind necessitates a careful meter reading. If the meter were pointed towards the sky, the face, which is shaded, would be underexposed, resulting in a silhouette. The reading should be taken off the face which would then be correctly exposed. There would be an extreme difference in value between the face and the sky areas, isolating the face from the background. With back lighting in portraiture, the subject has no need to squint. The soft light quality of shade is often quite desirable and effective.

In other situations, a back lit subject may not require the separation described in the previous paragraph. Detail in both the sky and face may be desirable. In this case, an average reading combined with the film's exposure latitude generally produces a satisfactory negative. A subject partially in shadow requires an average reading. The shadow and sunlit areas may be read (a close up reading), and the average of the two readings used for determining the exposure.

The determination of exposure in situations of extreme contrast requires careful meter readings. Present day films have an exposure latitude of four F/Numbers. As long as the readings are within this range, satisfactory exposures may be obtained. Some meters, for example the Weston Master, indicates this range with a U (underexposed) and O (overexposed) position. However, even with this wide exposure latitude, a correct reading is still essential.

2.   THE INCIDENT LIGHT METER

The other type of light meter, the incident light meter, measures the amount of light falling directly on the subject. The meter is held near the subject and pointed towards the camera. The indicated exposure is an average between the light and dark areas. See the following illustration.

The incident light meter was originally developed for color motion picture work, where an average exposure is generally required. It has also been used for commercial black and white photography, general color photography, and particularly for copying. Obtaining a reading with an incident light meter is quite different from obtaining one with a reflected light meter. Again, it is important to read carefully the instruction manual. The following are considerations to be aware of when using an incident light meter.

1.   An incident light meter is held close to the subject with the cell pointed towards the camera. If the cell points toward the subject, an incorrect exposure results.

2.   In making a reading with an incident light meter, it is important that the light which hits the light sensitive cell of the incident meter be of the same intensity as that falling upon the subject. If the subject is in sunlight, the reading must be obtained in sunlight.

3.   The shadow of the subject must never fall on the cell during the meter reading.

4.   A subject which is in partial shade, for example a person, requires that the cell of the meter be held half in shade and half in sunlight. In this manner an average reading may be obtained.

5.   In the case of back lighting, the incident light meter is held in the shadow of the subject, and pointed towards the camera.

The incident light meter gives an average reading for subjects which are often difficult to read with a reflected light meter. Two of these subjects include the beach and snow. They are very bright subjects, having a dominance of light tones. Usually there are areas of average and darker than average tonality as well. In this case, an average reading is needed but is difficult to obtain with a reflected light meter because of the fact that the reflected light meter is influenced by the dominance of light tones. A corrected exposure may be made, however, based upon guess work or previous experience.

In other situations the incident light meter's ability to determine accurate exposures is lacking. The incident light meter, which gives an average reading, is of little value when photographing objects darker or lighter than average. With extremely bright subjects, decreasing the exposure by one F/Number is usually sufficient. A dark subject sometimes presents more of a problem. It is difficult to judge whether an increase of one or two F/Numbers is sufficient. Using the reflected light meter, one is able to read these dark areas and to determine accurately the exposure.

The use of these two types of meters increases the accuracy and efficiency of exposure determination. Some situations are more easily handled with the reflected light meter, while others require the incident light meter, for best results. The average meter, although it may be designed for one method of reading, may be converted to the other method through the use of attachments. However, these attachments are generally awkward in operation.

SUBSTITUTE METER READING FOR REFLECTED LIGHT METERS

Copying paintings, drawings, and other two dimensional material usually requires a substitute meter reading. An average exposure is desirable and may be obtained easily by taking a reading from an 18% gray card. These cards are manufactured by Eastman Kodak and are readily available. The gray card is held against the material to be copied as the meter is pointed toward it at a very close range. The resulting exposure is an average exposure.

The substitute method of obtaining an exposure reading is also useful in photographing people. It is less conspicuous to read off the palm of one's hand than the subject's face. In this case, the indicated exposure reading must be increased by one F/Number. This allows for the relative difference between a skin tone and a gray card.

In other situations which are so dark that the meter hardly fluctuates, the use of a white card or piece of paper may make a reading possible. The meter is pointed toward the white card, and after the reading is made, the indicated exposure is increased by 2 1/2 F/Numbers. This increase in exposure compensates for the value difference between a white and a gray card.

BUILT-IN EXPOSURE METERS   (Automatic, Semi-automatic)

Cameras having built-in exposure meters are now numerous. The manner and degree of automatic operation varies greatly from one manufacturer to another. Some built-in exposure meters are fully automatic, whereas others are semi-automatic. The pros and cons of such an arrangement are debatable. The purpose of such an arrangement is to make the determination of exposure somewhat easier. One advantage of the built-in exposure meter is that it may not be left at home. Its disadvantage is that it is usually very small, which thereby reduces its accuracy. A camera with a built-in meter is also considerably more expensive than one without. However, the real problem of the built-in meter is that the camera must accompany the meter if repairs are necessary.

Photographing everyday situations may be accomplished quite easily with a camera having a built-in meter. However, in some situations the meter is unable to provide accurate exposure determinations. For example, a negative of a person wearing white clothing and standing in front of a large dark area might be overexposed, because of the dominance of the black which produces an exaggerated meter reading. A person in black clothes in front of a large white area might also be a problem. The white area would be exposed correctly, but the person would be represented as a silhouette.

Some of the automatic cameras have a "hold button." The hold button enables a close-up reading of the face to be made in order that the photographer may step back to photograph the subject. The hold button prevents the meter reading from changing as the photographer changes his position. Other automatic cameras may be switched to manual operation, which also allows for exposure correction. When using these cameras to photograph a landscape for example, the meter should be pointed directly down and that exposure retained. Otherwise the reading obtained by pointing toward the landscape will usually result in underexposure. An automatic camera which does not have a hold button or does not allow for manual operation may produce over or underexposed negatives.

EXPOSURE METERS (EXTINCTION)

The extinction meter is a visual exposure meter. As you look into it, you notice two values. These values are adjusted until they either match or blend together. An accompanying scale converts this adjustment into F/Number shutter speed combinations. These meters have been relatively cheap, but not very accurate. They have not taken into consideration the individual differences of the eye. Two different people may produce two different readings. The extinction type meter has generally been replaced by the more accurate photo-electric exposure meter.

EXPOSURE VALUE SYSTEM

The Exposure Value System is a recent innovation which combines and simplifies the operation of the F/Number with the shutter speed. In place of F/Number and shutter speed, the Exposure Value System is a combination of the two, offering a single number within the Exposure Value System. The Exposure Value System numbers range from 2 - 18, with 2 as a low reading. The relation between each number is either 1/2 or twice the exposure, depending on the way in which the scale is moved. For example, E.V. 9 (Exposure Value 9) provides twice the amount of exposure as E.V. 10. Recent exposure meters have an E.V.S. scale as well as the F/Number-shutter speed scales. After taking an exposure reading the camera may be set accordingly. The subject must be analyzed to determine whether a fast shutter speed or a great amount of depth of field is required. Because the shutter speed and F/Number are cross-coupled, any change in one automatically results in a change in the other. As a result, the exposure calculations are simpler and more consistent.

OUTDOOR AND AVAILABLE LIGHT EXPOSURE SUGGESTIONS

Outdoor exposures may be estimated through the use of the following chart. The chart recommends exposure settings for adjustable cameras, using different speed films on various types of days. Lighting conditions indicated below refer to the brightness of illumination from the sun. Every situation contains a mixture of light. Bright, average, and dark areas reflect different amounts of light. Most situations may be thought of as having average reflectance. One exception would be a bronze statue, as it would require more exposure because bronze is very dark. Another exception would be someone dressed in white at the beach. This subject would require less exposure because of its lightness.

The accuracy of the chart depends on how well the existing conditions match the examples. The exposure latitude of today's film also helps to lessen the possible margin of error. This chart is not intended to replace exposure meters. Instead, it attempts to serve as a guide if a meter is not available.

FILM	BRIGHT SUN Beach Snow	BRIGHT SUN Strong Shadows	LIGHT OVERCAST No Shadows	HEAVY OVERCAST Open Shade	DARK SHADE
Pan. - X (32 A.S.A.)	F/16 1/60	F/11 1/60	F/8 1/30	F/5.6 1/30	F/3.5 1/30
Ver. - Pan (125 A.S.A.)	F/16 1/250	F/11 1/250	F/8 1/125	F/8 1/60	F/5.6 1/30
Plus - X Pan (125 A.S.A.)	F/16 1/250	F/11 1/250	F/8 1/125	F/8 1/60	F/5.6 1/30
Tri - X Pan (400 A.S.A.)	F/22 1/250	F/16 1/250	F/11 1/125	F/8 1/125	F/8 1/30

INDOOR AND AVAILABLE LIGHT EXPOSURE SUGGESTIONS

The following exposure suggestions are to be used only as points of departure. Situations and lighting conditions vary to such an extent that definite exposure settings are impossible. The use of Tri - X (400 A.S.A.) film is suggested for all these situations.

INDOORS - AVAILABLE LIGHT

Moderately dim indoor locations with enough light to read a newspaper easily. Bus, railroad, airport terminals, many stores, darker classrooms, well-lighted restaurants, snack bars, etc.

1/30 at F/4

Bright indoor locations with light colored walls and ceilings. Modern kitchens, offices, banks, bright classrooms, photolab rooms, etc.

1/30 at F/5.6

Stage shows and plays.

1/30 at F/2.8 or F/4

OUTDOORS - AVAILABLE LIGHT

Brightness in night scenes varies considerably. Exposures are only approximated. In each situation, three different exposures should be made. With a few of the non-adjustable cameras, it is possible to make time exposures. These cameras have either a "B" or "T" setting. With the camera firmly braced or attached to a tripod, one is able to photograph at night.

SITUATION	ADJUSTABLE CAMERA	NON-ADJUSTABLE CAMERA
Wet streets, reflecting lights	2, 4, 8 seconds at F/5.6	30 - 45 seconds
City streets with snow	2, 4, 8 seconds at F/5.6	30 - 45 seconds
Neon and other electric lights	1/2 to 1 second at F/11	1 - 2 seconds
Fires, campfires, burning buildings	1/4, 1/2, 1 second at F/11	1 - 2 seconds
Street scenes with moving cars - streaks of light	8, 15, 30 seconds at F/11	1/2 - 1 minute
Average city street scene residential area	4, 8, 16 seconds at F/5.6	1 minute
Bright city street scene downtown area	1, 2, 4 seconds at F/5.6	30 seconds

LIGHT

Light is a form of energy which radiates in all directions from its source. It is only one of many different types of radiation and occupies a very small portion of the electromagnetic spectrum. Light radiating into space is partially reflected off objects. Reflected light is visible to the eye and camera. Light has certain qualities which directly affect the process of making photographs.

> Light can be *absorbed*.
> Light can be *reflected*.
> Light can be *diffused*.
> Light can be *refracted* (bent).

LIGHT CAN BE *ABSORBED*

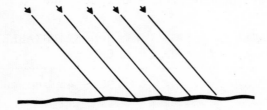

LIGHT CAN BE *REFLECTED*

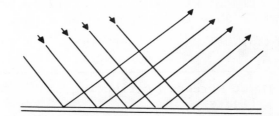

LIGHT CAN BE *DIFFUSED*

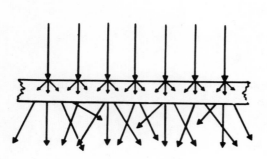

LIGHT CAN BE *REFRACTED*

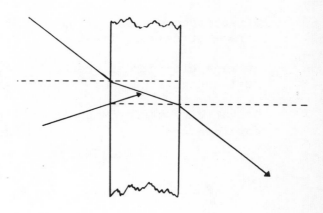

PICTORIAL QUALITIES OF LIGHT

Light, besides providing the mechanics for the image gathering properties
of photogtaphy, has a variety of qualities which directly influence the
imagery of a photograph. These qualities deal with how a subject appears
as it is illuminated by the various types of light, four in number, which
may be observed in nature or arranged in a studio. They are as follows:

      1.   Directional
      2.   Diffused
      3.   Edge
      4.   Silhouette

Directional light

Diffused light

Edge light

Silhouette

LIGHT, UPON ENTERING A PRISM, CHANGES DIRECTION (REFRACTION)

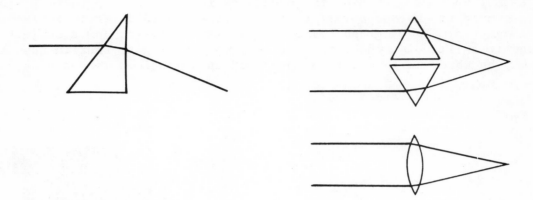

THE LENS

Prior to the use of glass for lenses, a *pinhole* was used. The pinhole effect was first noticed by an Arabian who observed an image of what was happening outside of his tent on the inside tent wall. He sought the reason for the phenomenon and found a tiny pinhole (literally the size of a pin prick) in the tent opposite from the image. The pinhole was, in effect, a crude lens and projected the image. The image formed by a pinhole is dark, not sharply defined, and possesses no real plane of focus. The first camera obscuras utilized pinholes which were eventually replaced with a lens. A lens improved the brightness of the image, made it sharper, and provided definite planes of focus.

Lenses are made in many different shapes, each having a unique characteristic. Basically, lenses may be classified as either positive or negative.

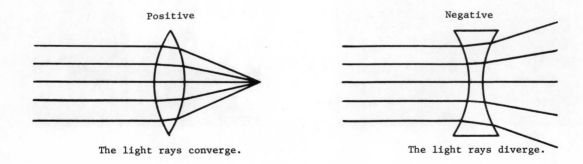

Positive — The light rays converge.

Negative — The light rays diverge.

The lens in a modern camera contains not one piece of glass, but several. Each piece of glass is called an *element*.

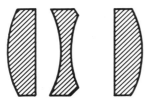 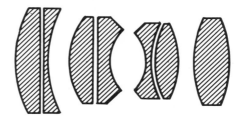

This lens has three elements.

This lens has seven elements.

An expensive lens may have up to eight elements. Inexpensive lenses have fewer. The shape, size and combination of elements are the factors in the designing of a lens.

FOCAL POINT

Light rays originating at infinity are parallel when they enter a lens.

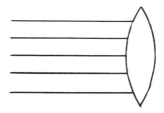

These parallel light rays are bent by the lens and converge on a common point.

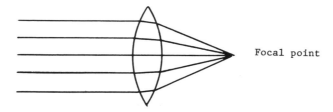

A thin lens causes light rays to converge at a farther point than a thick lens.

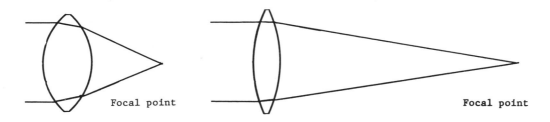

28

The point at which the parallel light rays converge, when focused at a point source of light at infinity, is the *focal point* of that particular lens.

FOCAL LENGTH

The distance between the lens and focal point, when focused at infinity, is the focal length of that particular lens. In photography, infinity means something two or three hundred yards distant. For example, light originating from an object at infinity is gathered by the lens, bent and converged at a point 12" from the lens. This particular lens has a 12" focal length.

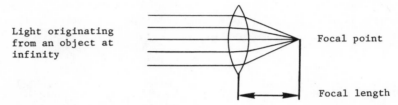

Light originating from an object at infinity

Focal point

Focal length

FOCUS - Circles of Confusion

The eye is constantly focusing and refocusing as we look from one object to another. It is a normal function of which we are unaware. The camera must do this mechanically.

The light from the sun, passing through a lens, will project a circle of light on a piece of paper. As the lens is moved closer or farther away from the paper, the circle will change in size. At the focal point (B), if held long enough in this position, the sun could ignite paper. The light from the sun is then in focus.

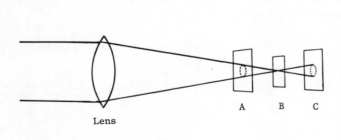

Lens

A   B   C

Only at point (B) is the light in focus. The out of focus circles, points (A) and (C) are called *circles of confusion.*

FOCUS - Objects at Different Distances

As long as we view or photograph objects at infinity, focusing is not a problem. But objects we observe are at different distances, some close, some intermediate and others far away. In order for a lens to focus on objects at different distances, the lens has to move back and forth from the point where the image is in focus.

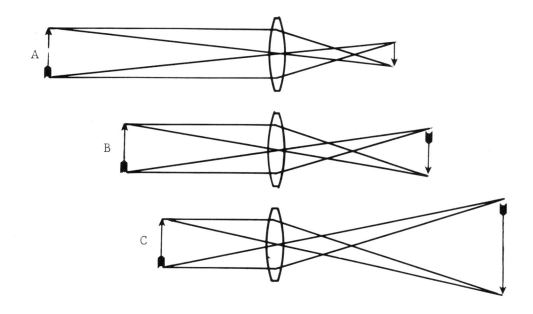

When focused on an object far away (sketch A), the distance between the lens and the point where the image is in focus is shorter than when focused on an object at an intermediate distance (sketch B). Compare sketch A to sketch B. When focused on a nearby object (sketch C), the distance between the lens and the point where the image is in focus is greater. The distance from the lens to the point at which an image is in focus is a variable depending on the distance of the object from the lens. Thus the lens must move back and forth from the point where the image is formed, in order for a camera to photograph objects at various distances.

The above sketches also illustrate how the image size changes as the distance between the subject and the lens varies. In sketch A, the image size (the arrow) is smaller due to the greater distance between the subject and the lens. In comparing sketch B to sketch A, the image size of B is larger because the lens is closer. The image size is largest in sketch C because the subject is closest to the lens.

The arrow, in addition to changing in size, is upside down on the film when an exposure is made. An image viewed on the ground glass of a view camera is also inverted. In fact, all negatives are made

30

with inverted images. This same phenomenon occurs in the human eye.
In the case of the eye, the brain turns an image right side up.

F/NUMBER FORMULA

A variety of different lens sizes necessitates an accurate method of
describing a lens' ability to gather light. It is a standard procedure in the categorization of all lenses to state this light
gathering ability numerically. The following formula may be used.

	F/N	Represents the light gathering ability of a lens
$F/N = \dfrac{F.L.}{D}$	D	Represents the diameter of the lens
	F.L.	Represents the focal length of the lens

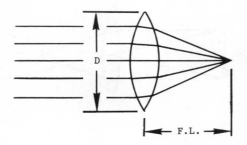

If you think of the F/Number as a fraction, the relationship between
the F/Number and its ability to gather light is easier to understand.
1/2 is larger than 1/8.

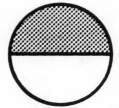

Similarly, F/2 is larger than F/8 and therefore gathers more light.
A common error is to think that F/2 is a smaller number than F/8 and
gathers less light. It does not.

F/NUMBER - Diameter of Lens

An F/Number has two variables, the diameter of the lens and the distance
the light must travel to the film. The F/Number formula is dependent
on each of these. The first example of this involves the diameter of
the lens. Two cameras, of the type in which the image may be seen on
the ground glass (i.e. two view cameras), are focused on the same subject. One camera has a much larger lens than the other. How would the
ground glass images differ in the two cameras?

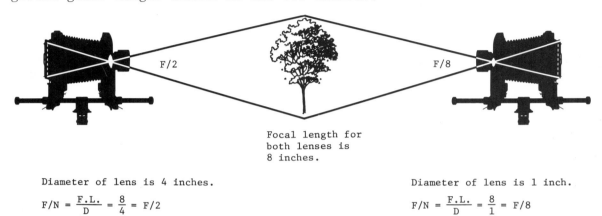

Focal length for
both lenses is
8 inches.

Diameter of lens is 4 inches.

$$F/N = \frac{F.L.}{D} = \frac{8}{4} = F/2$$

Diameter of lens is 1 inch.

$$F/N = \frac{F.L.}{D} = \frac{8}{1} = F/8$$

The camera with the larger lens, the F/2 lens, would have a brighter
image because of the lens' ability to gather more light. In practice,
this means that the camera with an F/2 lens (or larger) may be used to
photograph in dark situations. A non-adjustable camera has an F/11
or F/16 lens which makes it possible to photograph only on bright, sunny days. In photographic slang, a "large" lens is synonymous with a
"fast" lens. "Fast" cameras enable the photographer to take advantage
of available light and a variety of subjects.

The above example of the F/Number formula involves only the size of
the lens. The focal lengths of both the lenses is the same. Focal
length, which is the second variable, is illustrated in the following
example.

F/NUMBER - Focal Length of Lens

Two cameras, again of the type in which the image may be seen on the
ground glass, are focused on the same subject. Each lens has a different focal length.

32

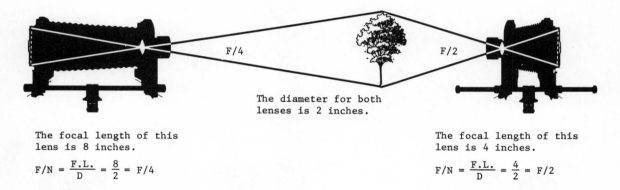

F/4

F/2

The diameter for both
lenses is 2 inches.

The focal length of this
lens is 8 inches.

$$F/N = \frac{F.L.}{D} = \frac{8}{2} = F/4$$

The focal length of this
lens is 4 inches.

$$F/N = \frac{F.L.}{D} = \frac{4}{2} = F/2$$

The camera with the 4" focal length would have the brighter image.
Both lenses are the same size, but one camera has a longer focal
length, hence a smaller F/Number.

In conclusion, the intensity of light in the exposure of the film
is dependent upon two factors, the diameter of the lens and the
focal length of the lens. This is designated by the F/Number and is
applicable to all lenses, regardless of their various sizes.

DIAPHRAGM - Function

The eye requires a certain amount of light for vision. In absolute
darkness there is no vision. Correspondingly, the eye cannot accommodate too much light. Excess brightness causes headaches and even
blindness. In situations between these two extremes a mechanism
controls the amount of light entering the eye. It is called the
iris. The iris is a device which opens and closes, dependent upon
the light intensity. It is an automatic function of which we are
unaware.

A certain amount of light is also necessary in using a camera. If
too little light enters the camera, film does not receive adequate
exposure and is often blank. If too much light enters the lens of
the camera, the resulting negative is overexposed and lacks detail.
Years ago the manner of controling the light entering a camera consisted of a number of pieces of metal, each with a different size
aperture.

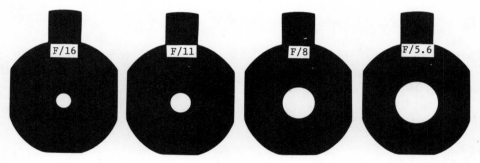

F/16   F/11   F/8   F/5.6

On an average day the F/11 aperture would be used. A dark day would require a F/8 or F/5.6 aperture because these apertures would allow more light to enter the lens. A very bright day would require a F/16 aperture. The photographer was then able to control the amount of light entering the camera's lens, taking into consideration the brightness of the day. This method worked well but, as materials improved, a more versatile system was required.

DIAPHRAGM - Description

The modern diaphragm, a series of tiny metal blades which open wide or close down to a small opening, is a clever device. An infinite variety of openings are possible. It became necessary to devise a system, the unit of measurement being the F/Number. As the diaphragm is opened or closed, the various openings are marked by F/Numbers.

F/1, F/1.4, F/2, F/2.8, F/4, F/5.6, F/8, F/11, F/16, F/22, F/32

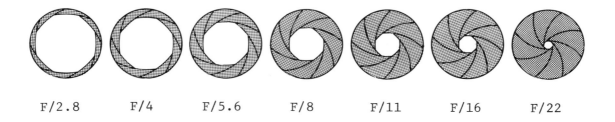

    F/2.8   F/4   F/5.6   F/8   F/11   F/16   F/22

As the above diagram illustrates, the aperture openings have a definate relationship to each other. F/8 allows one half the amount of light to enter the lens of the camera as does F/5.6; conversely, F/5.6 allows twice as much light to enter the lens as does F/8. The diaphragm is a standard means of controlling the amount of light entering any type of lens, regardless of size.

LENSES - TELEPHOTO, WIDE ANGLE

A lens on a camera is usually designed to photograph the same area that
we are able to see. For example, if we must stand ten feet from a subject
in order to see it in its entirety, the camera must also be ten feet from
the subject. The lens used in this example would be considered a "normal"
lens for that particular camera. A 50 mm lens is normal for a 35 mm
camera. An 8" X 10" camera requires a 12 inch lens. A normal focal
length for a given lens is usually the diagonal measurement of its
film size. The following is a list of normal focal lengths for
cameras using different size films.

```
        50 mm lens          -  35 mm roll film
        75 mm lens          -  120 roll film
        5 to 6 inch lens    -  4" x 5" sheet film
        12 to 14 inch lens  -  8" x 10" sheet film
```

A normal lens for one camera is not necessarily a normal one for another.
In fact, the opposite is often the case; a 12 inch lens is normal for an
8 x 10 inch camera, but is an extremely long lens for a 35 mm camera.

TELEPHOTO LENSES

Often the situation is such that a normal lens does not present the desired image in the camera's view finder. An obstacle or situation may
prevent the photographer from manipulating his distance to subject. For
example, to approach a wild animal is not only dangerous, it is also
awkward because of the possibility of the animal's sensing an intrusion.
Attempting to photograph this animal with a normal lens results in the
animal's being a very small object in the total scene. Enlarging a
tiny section of the negative is not a practical answer. In total, the
use of a telescope would be an advantage. The principle of magnification used in the telescope is also used in the telephoto lens.

Medium and high priced cameras have provisions for interchangeable lenses.
The normal lens may be removed, so that a longer one may be inserted. The
degree of magnification depends on the focal length of the lens. The longer
the focal length of the lens in relation to the normal lens, the greater
the degree of magnification.

In discussing the characteristics and qualities of lenses, the lenses
for a 35 mm camera will be used for an example. Lenses in the 85 - 105
mm range are very useful. They increase the image size and are, at the
same time, small. Many photographers prefer lenses in this range because they are able to photograph the subject from a slightly greater
distance. Portraits are ideal with these lenses because a normal lens
produces a slightly distorted image when it is used at close range.

The use of a lens twice the normal focal length (100 mm) doubles the image size. A 400 mm lens magnifies the image size by eight. In this case, a subject which is 80 feet away appears to be only 10 feet away. Thus, a 400 mm lens is often the practical answer for the wild game photographer. See the following illustration on the left.

The perspective in the above right photograph is compressed. There is little feeling of space between the objects in the scene. It has the quality of a mosaic or a paste-up, a quality of visual flatness. Often the photographer will purposely use this visual quality in his photographs to help give the subject a different appearance.

A long lens, because of its focal length, produces very little depth of field, even at small apertures. It allows photographs to be made with the background entirely out of focus and offers a means of separating objects optically, instead of by differences in tonal values.

Lenses for the 35 mm camera which exceed 200 mm are generally *telephoto lenses*. A telephoto lens is physically half the actual focal length of the lens and yet produces the same optical characteristics. This reduction in size enables long lenses to be slightly lighter and less cumbersome.

Atmospheric haze is often a problem when one uses a long telephoto lens, and requires that suitable filters be used. Orange, yellow and red filters offer different degrees of penetration of atmospheric haze. For ultimate penetration, infrared film and a deep red filter are necessary. Often, long lenses produce negatives with a lack of contrast. In this case a slower film may be used. Such a film has more contrast than a faster film. Another solution involves the underexposure overdevelopment technique. The subject may also be side-lighted in order to produce additional contrast.

Rangefinder cameras are not ideally suited for extremely long telephoto lenses. The rangefinder may not accommodate lenses of these
lengths. Expensive 35 mm rangefinder cameras may be converted to
single lens reflexes with expensive accessories in order to accommodate long lenses. However, they become rather bulky. Single lens
reflexes accomplish the same task without expensive and bulky accessories.

Telephoto lenses are quite susceptible to both camera and subject movement. A telephoto lens is generally rather slow. Few are faster than
F/4. Even if the telephoto lens were faster, the increase in actual lens
area would only make the lens heavier and bulkier. As a result, the long
telephoto lens requires the use of a fast shutter speed or a tripod.
Ideally, both should be used.

Recently, a supplementary lens system has appeared involving the use of
the *tele-extender*. After a tele-extender has been attached to the camera, the telephoto lens is fastened on to it. The use of the tele-extender
doubles the relative focal length of the lens. For example, a 200 mm lens
effectively becomes a 400 mm with the addition of the tele-extender. The
tele-extender usually cuts down on the relative sharpness of the image.
It involves a compromise between maximum quality and cost.

LENSES - WIDE ANGLE

The wide angle lens is the opposite of the long (telephoto) lens. The
camera with a normal lens may be the same distance from the subject as
the person is from the subject, and may cover the same area seen by the
person. The wide angle lens may cover that same area at a much closer
distance. If, for example, it was necessary for a camera with a normal
lens to be 10 feet from the subject in order for the subject to be photographed, it would be necessary for a camera with a wide angle lens to be
only seven feet from the subject in order to photograph that same subject.
This factor is especially important to the photographer who, because of
an obstruction, cannot stand far enough away from the subject to photograph it with a normal lens. The wide angle lens offers a means of
changing the photographer's relative distance to the subject without
actually moving. The wide angle lens, which has a short focal length,
produces a great amount of depth of field.

A wide angle lens produces a quality of imagery which the photographer
must consider. Perspective and proportion are quite different from that
seen by the eye, and the imagery has a round, fluid quality. A wide
angle lens having a long focal length (35 mm) does not produce as drastic a rendition as one having a short focal length (21 mm). See the
illustrations on the following page.

 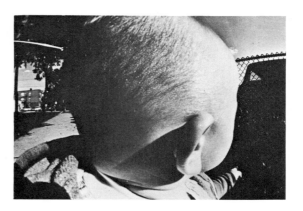

Because of its condition of perspective and proportion, the wide angle lens does not lend itself to portraiture. Using the wide angle lens, faces appear round and distorted, and generally unflattering.

The above right illustration was made with an extreme wide angle lens, a *fish eye*, which produces a rather bizzare visual effect. Everything appears circular, including the image format. Because this rendition of a subject is so strange, it may have a strong element of fantasy. This may be desirable for some situations. In general, however, the fish eye lens is designed for commercial and scientific photography.

The following chart and idagram indicate the angle of coverage of the various lenses for a 35 mm camera and the relationship of wide angle, normal, and telephoto lenses.

18	21 28 35	50 - 55	85 - 100	200 400 600
fish eye	wide angle	normal	medium	long lenses
			long lenses	Telephoto

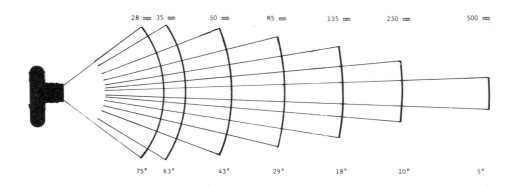

The use of different lenses enables the photographer to change his relative distance from the subject without actually changing his position. The illustration on the left shows how a subject changes as it is photographed with lenses ranging from a wide angle to a telephoto.

The illustration on the right shows how an object appears to change size as it is photographed with lenses of various focal lengths. The front sign is the same size throughout. Notice how the background white shapes change size.

CARE OF LENSES

The lens is made of glass and must be protected from scratches. These scratches reduce its effective sharpness. The use of a lens cap is suggested when carrying or storing the camera. When photographing, a sun shade not only helps cope with stray light, but also offers additional protection.

The lens must also be clean. Any dust, dirt, lint, or fingerprints reduces its sharpness. The cleaning of a lens requires care because the lens surface is easily scratched. The following items are needed for cleaning a lens:

1. Camel hair brush or an infant rectal syringe
2. Lens tissue
3. Lens cleaner (Kodak)

The camel hair brush is used for gently brushing away any dust, dirt, etc. which may be on the lens. An infant rectal or ear syringe may also be used to blow dust or dirt from the lens. The lens tissue is used to carefully and lightly wipe the lens in a circular motion. A scrubbing motion must never be used. Care is essential.

Any lens tissue other than that which is specified for photographic lenses should not be used. The lens tissue used for eye glasses is not recommended. This tissue often contains a cleaner which is harmful to the coating on a lens. The lens cleaner is especially useful if a fingerprint occurs on the lens. Because the cleaner is a solvent, it helps dissolve the oil from a fingerprint. As a result, less wiping is necessary.

DEPTH OF FIELD

Depth of field is the distance from the subject closest to the camera which is in focus to that farthest away which is also in focus. Consider the sketch on the following page.

40

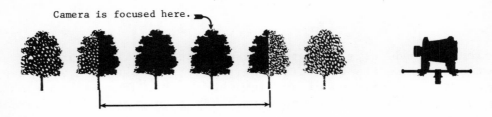

Camera is focused here.

Depth of field advances 1/3
and recedes 2/3.

The trees nearest to and farthest away from the camera are out of
focus. However, there are a number of trees between them which are
partially or totally in focus.

The photographer varies the depth of field by controlling the following three variables:

        1.   F/Number
        2.   Focal length of the lens
        3.   Distance from the subject

1. F/NUMBER - Determiner of Depth of Field

The F/Number, because of its aperture size, affects the depth of
field. In the following illustration the solid line represents
the path of light rays from a point on a subject which is in focus.
The broken line represents the path of light rays from a subject
farther away. Notice the images projected on the film. The solid
is a dot because it is in focus. The broken line is a circle of
confusion, because it is out of focus. The circle of confusion is
large when the diaphragm opening is wide, smaller when the diaphragm
opening is small. Thus the distant tree is in focus when the aperture is small. *The smaller the F/Number, the greater the depth of
field.*

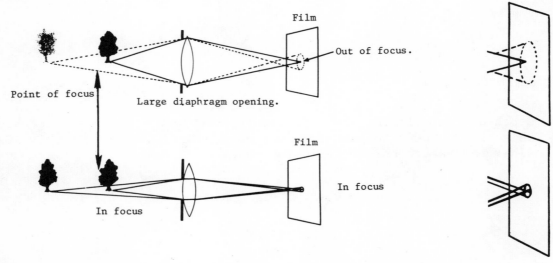

Film

Out of focus.

Point of focus

Large diaphragm opening.

Film

In focus

In focus

2. FOCAL LENGTH - Determiner of Depth of Field

A camera with a lens having a short focal length, for example a
movie camera, has a large depth of field. In fact, many movie
cameras have no provision for focusing. The large view cameras,
which require a long focal length lens, have little depth of field.
With the view camera, focusing is extremely critical.

There are three classifications of lenses when considering focal
length:

> The wide angle lens
> The normal lens
> The telephoto lens

The wide angle lens, having a short focal length, has a great depth
of field at a given F/Number. The normal lens, having a longer focal
length than the wide angle lens, has less depth of field. The telephoto lens, having a very long focal length, has very little depth
of field. *The shorter the focal length, the greater the depth of
field.*

3. DISTANCE FROM SUBJECT - Determiner of Depth of Field

The closer the lens is to the subject, the less the depth of field.
The following sketch illustrates what happens when focused upon
subjects at a close range. The in-focus image is a dot. The out-
of-focus image is a circle of confusion. When the subject is close
to the lens the circle of confusion is large, resulting in little
depth of field.

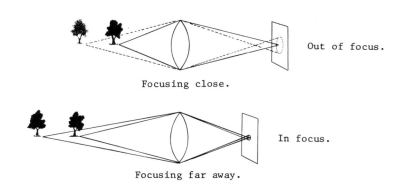

Focusing close.   Out of focus.

Focusing far away.   In focus.

The above sketch illustrates how the in-focus image and out-of-
focus image appear when focused on a subject far away. The difference between the in-focus image and the out-of-focus image is
considerably less in this situation which means that there is
more depth of field. *The farther the lens is from the subject,
(assuming the F/Number remains constant), the greater the depth
of field.*

THE CONTROL AND MANIPULATION OF DEPTH OF FIELD

The control and manipulation of depth of field is one of the most important considerations in photography. Depth of field enables the photographer to have control over areas both in and out of focus. In some situations, maximum depth of field may be desirable. In other situations no depth of field may be desirable. Determining how much depth of field is necessary is based on technical and esthetic considerations.

Background in focus.

Middleground in focus.

Foreground in focus.

Everything in focus.

VISUAL QUALITIES OF DEPTH OF FIELD

No depth of field.

Great depth of field.

The photographer, in this situation,
had the choice of great depth of field
or very little. He chose the latter.

The photographer had to sacrifice any
concern for depth of field in order to
obtain sufficient exposure.

DEPTH OF FIELD SCALES

The manner in which depth of field is indicated is different for each
type of camera and depends upon the camera's means of focus. The non-
adjustable (box) camera, which has no adjustment, has a fixed depth of
field. As long as the subject is at least five feet from the camera,
sharp focus is insured to infinity.

Other cameras have depth of field scales. These scales have two parts,
including F/Numbers and the camera-to-subject distance. The scale has
a center point which is indicated by the maximum F/Number for that particular lens. For example, see the following scale for a F/3.5 lens.

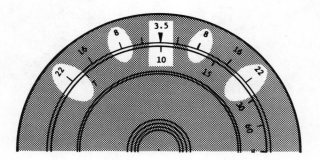

The succeeding F/Numbers are arranged on both sides of F/3.5. The distance from the camera to subject is moved along the F/Number scale and
indicates the resulting depth of field. Depth of field is dependent
upon the focal length of the lens, the F/Number, and the distance from
the camera to the subject. Because the same lens is used throughout
this example, the focal length does not vary. The subject-to-camera
scale is moved along the F/Number scale.

The above diagram gives an example. Opposite F/3.5 on the F/Number
scale is the number ten, which means that the camera is focused on a
subject at a distance of ten feet. Depending on the F/Number used,
the depth of field varies. The number opposite the respective F/Num-
ber indicates the limits of the depth of field. For example, at F/8
the depth of field is from eight to thirteen feet. If F/22 were used,
the depth of field would be considerably larger. Any object from roughly six and three quarter feet to twenty-three feet from the camera
would be in sharp focus.

Depth of field scales are invaluable aids for the photographer using
cameras in which the depth of field may not be visually observed. The
manner of presentation of depth of field scales varies from camera to

camera. They are usually on a curved plane because the lenses are cylindrical. Older cameras and press cameras have the depth of field scales which are flat and located on the lens bed.

The use of depth of field scales does not indicate visually how a subject will be rendered which is partially or completely out of focus. With experience, it is possible to make predictions. However, this is not as desirable as the actual visualization of the subject.

All cameras, with the exception of the view cameras, have depth of field scales. Their frequency of use again depends upon how the camera is focused. All manual distance adjustment cameras make use of these scales, including the rangefinder cameras. Although it makes use of ground glass focusing, the twin lens reflex camera offers a scale in order to indicate the depth of field. The single lens reflex also offers a depth of field scale. However, the scale is not as necessary to the single lens reflex cameras as it is to other types of cameras because of the fact that depth of field may actually be seen through the lens.

ZONE FOCUSING

The use of zone focusing is particularly useful for cameras which have depth of field scales. It is also useful if the subject is moving so fast that it is difficult to focus (candids, sports, etc.). The camera is set at the distance the subject will be from the camera. The depth of field scales may be checked in order to see which areas of the subject will be in focus. The exposure may then be made when the subject enters the area of sharp focus.

HYPERFOCAL FOCUSING

The use of the hyperfocal focusing technique produces the maximum depth of field for a given F/Number. It applies to outdoor exposures which require that the aperture be closed down. It also applies to objects in the subject which are in the middle to far distant range. When photographing a scene at infinity, the normal habit is to have the focusing scale set at infinity. For example, with a twin lens reflex the depth of field is from twenty-five feet to infinity at F/16. See the diagram on the following page.

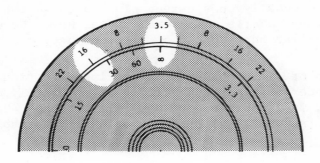

Anything closer than 25 feet is out of focus. The use of the hyperfocal
focusing technique increases this relative amount of depth of field. Instead of setting the focus at infinity, the focus may be set at the opposite of the F/Number being used (F/16 in this particular example). See
the following diagram.

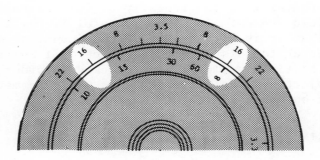

Notice opposite the F/16 on the distance scale that 13 feet is then
indicated as the near limit of the depth of field. Thus the use of
hyperfocal focusing increased the relative depth of field by 12 feet.

THE SHUTTER

The exposures for the first photographs were very long, often several
minutes. This fact limited the choice of subjects to be photographed.
Street scenes, still lifes and landscapes were possible because they
were generally quite stationary. Portraiture was not possible, and
was a real commercial hindrance. One of the first people to appear
in a photograph was a gentleman who happened to stop on a busy Paris
street in order to have his shoes shined. Horses, carriages and pe-
destrians passed as he remained in that one position. As a result,
the people and the carriages were not recorded, but the man was.

Gradually, as the sensitivity of the materials increased and the lenses
improved, the exposures shortened. These shortened exposures made
portraits possible. This marked the beginning of photography as a commercial business. However, portraits were made under rather difficult
circumstances. The subject had to remain perfectly still for seconds,
which was very hard. Numerous devices such as neck clamps were employed
to hold the people stationary. Faces were often covered with white
powder in order to obtain shorter exposures. Other photographers used
mirrors to reflect the sunlight.

The lens had a cover to protect it as well to provide a means by
which the photographer could control the length of exposure. In
practice, the cover was moved in order for the photographer to
choose his imagery. The cover was then placed over the lens, preventing any light from entering the lens as he placed the film holder
in position. The exposure was determined by the length of time the
cover was off the lens. This was a somewhat crude system, but was
satisfactory as long as the exposure was several seconds. However,
as the exposures were shortened to parts of a second, this system
proved inadequate.

The shutter is a device which opens and closes in controllable
amounts of time and is the means by which exposures are made.
Numerous ideas and types have evolved. Some shutters are based
upon a taut spring and gear mechanism which opens and closes a number of tiny metal leaves. Another type of shutter, the
focal plane shutter as the name implies, is a shutter which
operates at the focal plane. It involves the use of a cloth or
metal curtain which travels past the film plane at different
speeds. It provides a full range of shutter speeds. The focal
plane shutter and the taut spring mechanism are the two types
of shutters in general use today.

SHUTTER SPEEDS

The following are the common shutter speeds: 1, 1/2, 1/4, 1/8, 1/15, 1/30, 1/60, 1/125, 1/250, 1/500 and 1 /1000 of a second. They are fractions; 1/30 of a second means that the shutter is opened for that amount of time.

The shutter speed should always be set on one speed or another. It should be on either the 1/125 or the 1/60, and not between them. The shutter does not function in the same manner as the aperture; it is not continuous. *An attempt to use a shutter speed between two settings may harm the shutter mechanism.* Results may also be inaccurate and inconsistent.

B and T

In addition to a full range of shutter speeds, a shutter usually has a "B" or "T" setting. Sometimes the shutter offers both of these. The "B" and "T" settings are used for time exposures. They allow the shutter to open for the desired amount of time. The "B", which is an abbreviation for bulb, keeps the shutter open as long as the shutter release is pressed. When it is released, the shutter closes. This setting is especially suited for short time exposures of one to thirty seconds. The "T", which is the abbreviation for time, is ideally more suitable for very long time exposures, including thirty seconds or more. As the shutter release is pressed, the shutter opens. It remains open for an indefinite amount of time, until it is pressed again. In summary, "B" may be used for short time exposures, while "T" may be used for long time exposures.

Time exposures require a firm support in order to eliminate camera movement. A tripod or an improvised support is necessary for all exposures *longer than 1/30 of a second*. Often a fence, tree, chair, hand railing, etc. will suffice if a tripod is not available.

A cable release is also necessary for time exposures. The hand, while holding the shutter release during the exposure, often shakes the camera. The cable release, which is a flexible extension between the hand and the camera, eliminates any such movement. The use of a cable release is strongly recommended for all time exposures. Cable releases are inexpensive and easily adaptable to most cameras.

The majority of cameras manufactured in recent years have only a "B" setting. With very long time exposures, there is a tendency for one to relax or change the position of his fingers, thereby releasing the pressure. As a result, the shutter may close prematurely, making the exposure considerably shorter. A locking cable release helps to eliminate this problem.

SHUTTER SPEED - F/Number Relationship

Everytime the shutter speed is changed, the F/Number must also be
changed in order to maintain correct exposure. Consecutive shutter
speeds have the same relationship to each other as consecutive
F/Numbers have, that is, each is twice the amount of the one pre-
ceding, or, vice versa, each is half the amount of the next largest.
Thus the exposure may be consistent, regardless of whether or not the
F/Numbers or shutter speeds are changed. See the following:

#1	#2	#3	#4	#5
F/5.6	F/8	F/11	F/16	F/22
1/500	1/250	1/125	1/60	1/30

All of the five examples above produce the same exposure because of
the fact that one change is compensating for another. But other
characteristics become evident in the differences in depth of field
and ability to stop motion. Compare example #1 to #5. Example #1
stops motion at 1/500 but has little depth of field (F/5.6). Example
#5 is the opposite. It has great depth of field (F/22), but 1/30
does not stop very fast action. It is impossible to have great
depth of field and yet be able to stop the fastest action. Example
#3 is a compromise. There is a reasonable amount of depth of field
with a fast enough shutter speed (1/125) to stop the action. When
photographing, the situation must be analyzed and the proper considerations made.

PHOTOGRAPHING MOVING OBJECTS

The shutter, while controlling the length of exposure, has the ability to stop motion. In order to stop fast action, such as the action
of a car in motion, shutter speeds of 1/250 or 1/500 of a second are
necessary. The shutter also has the ability to emphasize the motion
of a fast moving car. This may be accomplished by using a slow shutter speed, such as 1/60 of a second, thereby exaggerating the motion.
A moving subject, photographed with a slow shutter speed, has a fluid
quality. The image appears to spread across the picture plane. For
many situations, this quality is quite exciting. These shutter speeds
express motion better than the frozen expression of motion of the
fast shutter speeds. The degree of fluidness is dependent upon the
speed of the subject as well as the shutter speed. There is no formula. When photographing in this manner, the end results can not
always be previsualized. It is advisable to make many exposures
with variations of shutter speeds. Accidents happen and may be utilized. Studying the results provides a background for future applications.

RELATION OF SHUTTER SPEED TO MOVING OBJECTS

Fast shutter speed.   Slow shutter speed

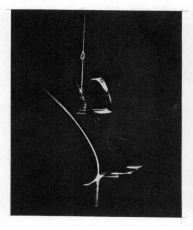

A spinning wire sculpture photo-
at various shutter speeds.

Fast shutter speed.   Slow shutter speed.

The photographer, in analyzing the situation and choosing a suitable shutter speed-F/Number combination, must consider the following four variables:

1. The speed of the subject
2. The angle and direction of the subject
3. The distance from the subject to the camera
4. Exposure considerations

1. THE SPEED OF THE SUBJECT

A fast-moving subject requires a faster shutter speed than a stationary subject. For instance, a moving vehicle requires a shutter speed of about 1/250 or 1/500 of a second to stop the motion, whereas a rock in a meadow may be photographed at a much slower speed.

2. THE ANGLE AND DIRECTION OF THE SUBJECT IN RELATION TO THE CAMERA

A subject moving directly across the field of vision of the camera requires a faster shutter speed (1/500 or 1/1000 of a second) than one coming towards or going away from the camera (1/125 or 1/250 of a second).

3. THE DISTANCE FROM THE SUBJECT TO THE CAMERA

The farther the subject is from the camera, the less pronounced is its speed. For instance, a distant, fast-moving subject may be photographed at 1/60 of a second. When it approaches the camera, it must be photographed at 1/250 or 1/500 of a second.

4. EXPOSURE CONSIDERATION

As the shutter speed is changed, the F/Number must also be changed in order to maintain a correct exposure.

There are two additional techniques which sometimes influence the photographing of moving subjects:

1. Peak of Action
2. Panning

1. PEAK OF ACTION

Sometimes there is a "peak of action," during which the subject is momentarily motionless (for example, a diver). With practice this split second may be photographed even with a relatively slow shutter speed.

2. PANNING

Using the panning technique, the camera is moved in an arc, paralleling the motion of the subject, thus reducing the difference in speed between the camera and subject. When one is using a non-adjustable camera, panning enables the camera to stop motion. The background usually has a fluid quality which isolates the subject.

FILM

The first attempts to capture an image with light-sensitive materials were based on a visual process. The experimenters exposed a light-sensitive material until an image became visible. These first efforts were futile because the development of these images could not be stopped. Instead, the images eventually turned black.

Daguerre succeeded where the others failed and produced permanent images. His process consisted of coating a metal plate with a light-sensitive silver compound. The exposure of this silver compound formed a *latent image*. This latent image was invisible and remained invisible until it was subjected to certain chemicals. Thus, the image became visible upon development, instead of upon direct exposure. The development of a latent image is the principle upon which photography is now based.

The exposure with the early processes was critical, because the material exposed in the camera became the finished product. These processes also did not lend themselves to duplication. Each photograph was unique and a separate entity.

The negative-positive principle which evolved from its predecessors provides greater flexibility. The negative, because it is an intermediate product provides considerable exposure latitude, as well as allowing duplicates to be made easily and economically.

DESCRIPTION

The films used today are quite different from their predecessors, the tin and glass plates. Modern films are complex. Every roll or sheet of film has the following five layers:

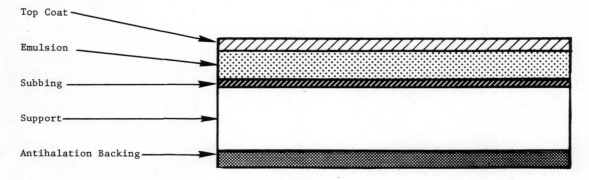

TOP COAT

The top coat is a protective layer of hard gelatin which helps to protect the *emulsion* from scratches.

EMULSION

The emulsion is a layer of gelatin which contains light sensitive silver. Upon development, this silver turns black in proportion to the amount of exposure.

SUBBING

The subbing is a special glue-like gelatin which adheres the emulsion to the support.

SUPPORT

The support is a transparent, strong and flexible acetate material.

ANTIHALATION BACKING

The antihalation backing is a coating of dye which is dissolved by the hypo (fix). Its purpose is to prevent light from reflecting off the support or back of the camera, while exposing the film. If reflections were not eliminated by this antihalation backing, bright areas on the film would have halos around them, reducing the sharpness of the image.

CHARACTERISTICS

Film has four basic characteristics:

1. Color Sensitivity
2. Contrast
3. Film Speed - A.S.A.
4. Grain

1. COLOR SENSITIVITY

Years ago film was not sensitive to all colors. At one time it was difficult to obtain clouds in a photograph because films were oversensitive to blue. The resulting negative was opaque in the cloud area because it was overexposed. The positive print showed the sky as totally white. These early films were *orthochromatic* because they were not sensitive to red and were oversensitive to blue. The following illustrations show the difference between an orthochromatic and *panchromatic* rendition of a subject.

Orthochromatic rendition.

Panchromatic rendition.

The orthochromatic rendition is false and an exaggerated one. In actuality, the barn is red. Here it appears almost black. With the panchromatic rendition the barn appears gray. This is a more truthful rendition of the subject. Panchromatic film is sensitive to all colors, and will record them in their proper shade of gray.

2. CONTRAST

The contrast of a film describes the film's ability to record values of gray (white through gray to black). Some films are contrasty and record only a limited number of values, while other films are not as contrasty and record a greater number of values.

3. FILM SPEED - A.S.A.

Every type of film is given a film speed of an A.S.A. or Din. number indicating the film's degree of sensitivity. The A.S.A. number is established through tests by the American Standard Association. The Din. number is used primarily in Europe.

                    400 A.S.A. - Fast Film   - 27 Din.
                    160 A.S.A. - Medium Speed Film- 23 Din.
                     50 A.S.A. - Slow Speed Film - 10 Din.

A fast film has a high A.S.A. number, for example, 400 A.S.A. - 27 Din. and is needed for low light levels in available light situations. A medium speed film, for example, 160 A.S.A. - 23 Din. is needed for average daylight situations, and a slow film, for example, 50 A.S.A. - 10 Din. is needed for extremely bright situations such as at the beach or scenes covered with snow.

4. GRAIN

During the development of film microscopic particles of silver clump together. These particles are most noticeable in large magnifications of the negative. Because of this, the resulting prints are called *grainy*. A print becomes too grainy when the texture of the grain prevents the image from being sharp. Often the quality of a photograph suffers if the grain becomes excessive.

High speed films are grainier than medium or slow speed films, and should be used in situations which are too dark for the use of slower speed films.

TYPES OF FILM

There are many brands of film (both domestic and foreign) on the market. It is best to use film from one manufacturer at first, rather than constantly changing from one brand to another. Also, it is advisable to avoid "surplus bargains" because such film is usually out of date. The following is a list of films manufactured in the United States:

EASTMAN KODAK		ANSCO	
Panatomic - X	32 A.S.A.	Verispan	125 A.S.A.
Verichrome Pan.	125 A.S.A.	Super Hypan	500 A.S.A.
Plus - X	125 A.S.A.		
Tri - X	400 A.S.A.		
Royal - X	1250 A.S.A.		

Eastman Kodak Panatomic - X (32 A.S.A.)

Available in most roll and sheet film sizes. It has a slow A.S.A. number and has the finest grain. This film produces great detail, providing the light level is sufficiently bright. Panatomic - X may be used in a non-adjustable camera in bright situations, such as the beach.

Eastman Kodak Verichrome Pan (125 A.S.A.)

Available only in roll film sizes with the exception of 35 mm. It is a medium speed film, has fine grain, and is ideal for the non-adjustable camera in an average situation.

Eastman Kodak Plus - X (125 A.S.A.)

Available in 35 mm, 120 and 620 roll film and sheet film. It has fine grain with adequate film speed for most situations. Plus - X in 120 size is usually unavailable at the corner drug store because it is used primarily by commercial photographers. However, it is readily available in 35 mm, and is the best film for general use.

Eastman Kodak Tri - X (400 A.S.A.)

Available in all roll film sizes and sheet film. It is a fast film which has a coarser grain than the previously mentioned slower films. Tri - X film is needed for available light situations using 35 mm, or on very dark days using a non-adjustable camera. Tri - X is not a general purpose film. It is used only in situations where the slower speed films are not adequate.

Ansco Verispan (125 A.S.A.)

Available in all roll film sizes and 35 mm. It is similar to Kodak Plus - X.

Super Hypan (500 A.S.A.)

Available in all roll film sizes and 35 mm. It is similar to Kodak Tri - X.

EXPOSURE - FILM

The deposit of silver on a negative is directly proportional to the amount of light hitting the film. The relative thickness of this deposit is called the *density*. The term density is a means of describing whether a negative is properly exposed, overexposed, or underexposed. A properly exposed negative has an ample deposit of blackened silver particles on its emulsion, and therefore, has good density. An overexposed negative has an excess of blackened silver particles, and has too much density. This negative is frequently called a thick negative. An underexposed negative does not have an ample deposit of blackened silver particles, and has too little density. This may be called a thin negative.

A cross-section of these three basic types of negatives is greatly magnified in the following illustration. The difference in density among them is apparent.

Normal esposure.   Overexposure.   Underexposure.

The correctly exposed negative has a full range of tones and produces a natural rendition of the subject. The overexposed negative contains areas which are "blocked-up." A blocked-up area is so dense that light is not able to penetrate through it. These areas appear stark white on a print and contain no detail. A *highlight* is also such an area, but is considered smaller in size. A blocked-up area is usually detrimental to the quality of the finished print. A highlight, on the other hand, is desirable because it gives a print a sparkling quality within its tonal range. A thin or underexposed negative has a pale, transparent quality. A full tonal range is lacking; there is very little difference between the white and black areas. A technically poor negative never yields a satisfactory print.

FILM-TYPES, LOADING INTO DEVELOPING TANK

Present day film, because it is sensitive to all light, must be developed in total darkness. Consequently, film may only be removed from its cartridge or separated from its paper backing in total darkness. There are three basic arrangements of roll film and each has its own unique characteristics. These are:

1. Roll Film (120, 620, 127, etc.)
2. 35 mm Film
3. Drop-in Cartridge (Instamatic)

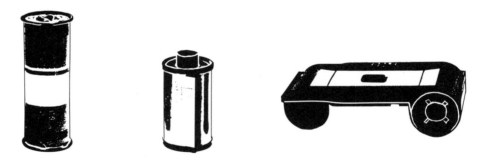

1. ROLL FILM

Roll Film (120, 620, 127, etc.) is available in many sizes. Each roll of film includes the spool, the film, and the paper backing.

The opaque paper backing is wrapped with the film around the spool, and prevents the film from being exposed while the camera is loaded or unloaded. It also acts as the *leader* which guides the film through the camera. The paper backing is also numbered which helps to prevent an overlapping of exposures when the film is advanced from one exposure to the next. Numbers may be viewed through the red opening which is in the back of an inexpensive camera. Expensive cameras do not make use of this visual observation, and as a result, the film advance is often automatic.

As an exposed roll of film is unrolled in total darkness, the film may be found. The film curls as it is separated from the paper backing and should only be handled by the edges in order to prevent finger-printing. Tape, which attaches the film to the paper backing, must be removed from the film. If it is not, tape may adhere to other areas of the film. Should this happen, the tape prevents these areas from being developed.

2. 35 mm FILM

Because it is motion picture film, 35 mm film includes sprocket holes. In the camera, these sprocket holes intermesh in a gear mechanism which operates the exposure counter, thus eliminating the necessity of ob-serving the numbers through the red window. Since 35 mm film comes in a cartridge, it does not require a paper leader. The actual film is trimmed for a short length enabling it to be attached to the take-up spool. The film, after being exposed, is rewound into the film car-tridge prior to removing it from the camera.

In order to process 35 mm film, it must be removed from the cartridge. This must be done in *total darkness*. A bottle opener may be used to remove the flanges from the ends of the cartridge. See the illustration below.

The spool of film is then removed from the cartridge. The "tongue" portion of the film must be cut off, as well as the end of the film which is joined to the spool. See the above right illustration.

3. DROP-IN CARTRIDGE (INSTAMATIC)

The drop-in cartridge (Instamatic) is a new film system which has been introduced by Eastman Kodak. Film is contained in a plastic cartridge. After exposure, this plastic cartridge must literally be ripped apart in order to obtain the film. Again, this must be done in *total dark-ness*. As the cartridge is gripped with both hands and twisted, it breaks in half. The exposed film may be found in the larger section of the cartridge. This section may, in turn, be opened by a prying action. Usually this may be accomplished without too much difficulty. After this section has been opened, the film may be separated from the paper backing.

Drop-in cartridge (Instamatic) film is the same width as 35 mm film. It is also loaded onto the developing reel in a manner similar to the one used for 35 mm film. However, the manner of loading the film onto the reel depends upon the manufacturer. The instructions which accompany the reel should be read and followed carefully.

FILM PROCESSING - DESCRIPTION

The development of film is a very important part of the photographic process. Because film development is a chemical process, it involves a definite procedure which must be carefully followed. Any deviation or mistake in this process affects, and perhaps destroys, the technical quality of a negative. The negative, in turn, determines the quality of the resulting print.

DEVELOPING TANKS - ROLL FILM

Roll film may be developed very easily by using a developing tank. The tank consists of three parts, the tank, the reel and the lid. There are many brands and types of developing tanks on the market. The cheapest are made of plastic and have a reel which is adjustable for most sizes of film. Film size 120, which has the largest width in roll film, requires that the sections of the reel be spread as far apart as possible. On the other hand, 35 mm film requires that these two sections be as close together as possible.

The manner of loading the film onto the reel varies from manufacturer to manufacturer. Many of the older or "bargain" plastic reels do not properly accommodate present day thin films. In such a case, film does not load properly and often wrinkles. The Ansco-matic tank (an Ansco product) has a very simple method of loading film onto the reel. It works on a ratchet mechanism which has produced little trouble for beginning photographers. The main difficulty with the Ansco-matic tank involves the fact that the reels must be perfectly dry before they may be reused. The tank shatters easily when dropped, and does not readily accommodate a thirty-six exposure role of 35 mm film. Nikor, another type of developing tank, is made of stainless steel. Because a Nikor reel is not adjustable, a separate reel is needed for each film size. This type of tank is more expensive than the plastic tank, but is, in many ways, superior. A Nikor tank and reel will not shatter if dropped. Nikor also provides better agitation. Finally, there is no need for the reel to be perfectly dry before it may again be used. Nikor developing tanks are available in different sizes, allowing for more than one roll of film to be processed at one time. The investment in a stainless steel developing tank and reel is a wise one for the serious photographer.

The loading of film onto the developing reel is important. If the reel is improperly loaded, areas of the film may stick together and not receive proper development. It is advisable for the beginning photographer to practice loading with old film in order to gain competence.

When using an Ansco-matic tank there is the danger of the formation of air bubbles on the film, especially 35 mm. To reduce the danger, it is usually helpful to fill the developing tank with developer. Then with the room lights out, the film may be loaded onto the reel. As the loaded reel is inserted into the tank, it should be lifted up and down to dislodge any air bubbles. As soon as the lid is secure, the room lights may be turned on and development continued in the normal manner.

The development of film consists of subjecting the film to the following chemicals:

> Developer
> Water Rinse or Stop Bath
> Hypo (fix)
> Wash
> Wetting Agent

DEVELOPER

The emulsion contains tiny particles of silver which are called *silver halides*. These silver halides form a latent image when exposed to light. The latent image becomes visible when the developer turns the exposed silver halides to blackened particles of silver. These blackened particles of silver clump together during development to form the photographic image.

The number of film developers on the market is rather confusing. The advantages of one over another are, in many ways, a matter of opinion or preference. However, in general, there are three types of film developers. They are:

> Fine Grain Developers (Compensating)   T.E.C.
> All purpose, general use developers   U.F.G. – Microdol-X
> High energy developers   Acufine

The maximum in quality may be obtained by using a fine grain film, such as Panatomic-X, with a fine grain or compensating developer, such as T.E.C. For general use, Plus-X or Verichrome Pan film in combination with U.F.G. film developer is suggested. In situations which have a very low light level, a high energy developer such as Acufine may be used with Tri-X Pan film.

The above three developers are a suggestion and are by no means the rule. The beginning photographer has the tendency to try them all at once and, as a result, acquires no competence. Developers have a way of appearing on the market, becoming popular, and then fading away. The three developers mentioned here are popular and have been in use for some time.

In many situations where film developing chemicals are furnished, a
more economical developer than those mentioned above is necessary.
D-76, an Eastman Kodak product, is such a developer. It is not
ideal for available light photography and will not produce the finest
grain with slow films. However, for average photographic situations,
D-76 is a good general purpose developer. Its availability in bulk
sizes is also a consideration in a situation in which a large volume
of work is produced. Depending on the type of film used, D-76 is
often diluted for use and then discarded.

The use of sheet film and its manner of development also affects the
choice of a developer. U.F.G. developer can be used for both roll and
sheet film. The developing time for U.F.G. is ample for the tray
method of developing sheet film. Other developers, such as D-76, require a longer developing time, which is often desirable if other
methods of developing, such as nitrogen burst, are used. In the development of sheet film, the use of nitrogen burst and film hangers also
requires that the developing time be slightly longer.

Many developers have a replenisher system; that is, a certain amount
of developer replenisher is added to the developer every time a roll
of film is developed. This system allows for the development of a
greater number of rolls in a given amount of solution.

TIME - TEMPERATURE CHART

Developing time is a variable depending upon the type of film used
and the temperature of the developer. As long as the developer is
within a certain temperature range (68° - 75°F.), a specific developing time is required for each individual temperature. The *time -
temperature chart* which follows indicates developing times for different temperatures. However, the times for the different temperatures
are blank in order to accommodate your specific film and development. It
is important not to attempt to develop film outside of the indicated
temperature range. Warming or cooling the developer to a slight degree
may be necessary. However, it is usually easier to vary the developing
time than the temperature of the developer. A time temperature chart
is usually supplied with the instructions which accompany the developer.

Some developers are diluted with water, used once, and then discarded.
This usually applies to Pan-X and Plus-X in 35 mm size, used with certain developers. It is the reason for the distinction between roll
film and 35 mm on the chart, even though the type of film is the same.

Time-Temperature Chart

The following chart applies only to _____ film developer.

FILM		68°	70°	72°	75°
Panatomic-X	35 mm	___	___	___	___
	Roll film	___	___	___	___
Verichrome Pan	All film	___	___	___	___
Plus-X	35 mm	___	___	___	___
	Roll film		___	___	___
Tri-X	All film	___	___	___	___

TEMPERATURE OF THE CHEMICALS

The temperature of the solutions must be within a certain range (68° – 75°F.). If the temperatures of the solutions are out of the indicated range, warming or cooling is necessary. The rinse and wash water must also be within this range of temperature. Subjection of film to drastic changes in temperature causes excess grain, and in extreme cases, *reticulation*. Reticulation is literally the physical cracking or wrinkling of the emulsion. It is fatal, ruining the negatives.

CHECKING THE DEVELOPER FOR CONTAMINATION

Chemicals for developing film must be used in the proper order and kept free from contamination. Some schools make use of a community type of system for chemical distribution. For instance, when a student is finished with a particular chemical, he pours it back into a central container. If a student happens to pour hypo (fix) into the developer by accident, the developer is no longer good. It is unfortunate that this is not evident until another student attempts to develop his film. Film which is developed in contaminated developer is perfectly blank and is a total loss. To help prevent this from occuring, it is important to check the developer for contamination. A small piece of *litmus* paper may be inserted into the developer. If the litmus turns bright green, the developer is free from contamination. If, on the other hand, the litmus paper turns orange, the developer is contaminated.

> *Kelly Green* – Non-contaminated
> *Orange* – Do not use.

The litmus paper used for this test has a pH range of two to ten. It is commercially available from chemical and science supply companies. The litmus test requires only a few seconds, and is of great value in preventing mistakes.

AGITATION DURING DEVELOPMENT

It is important that the film is agitated while it is in each of the chemicals. Agitation of the film in the developer is critical. Using the Nikor or Ansco-matic tank, film should be agitated vigorously for the first 30 seconds, and then 5 seconds every 30 seconds thereafter for the entire developing period. Insufficient agitation may result in the presence of *air bubbles*. Air bubbles are literally tiny bubbles of air which adhere to the emulsion. As a result of this adhesion, the area of the emulsion covered by the bubble does not develop. This area appears as a clear area on the resulting negative, and a black spot on the resulting print. Some developing tanks, for example, the Ansco-matic, only allow for a rotating type of agitation. These tanks are more susceptible to air bubbles than the Nikor tanks which may be turned upside down.

Excess agitation is also undesirable, as it may cause streaks to appear on the negative. Many students spin the agitator in the Anscomatic developing tanks constantly. As a result, negatives are both overdeveloped and uneven. Agitation in solutions which follow the developer is less critical, but is still important.

WATER RINSE OR STOP BATH

The water rinse or stop bath removes the excess developer from the film before it is placed in the hypo. The prepared stop bath may be used for a number of rolls of film.

HYPO (FIX)

The hypo (fix) stops all development and removes the unexposed silver deposits, insuring the permanence of the image. It contains a hardening agent which makes the emulsion less susceptible to scratches and is usually more concentrated than that which is used for paper. Concentrated liquid hypo (fix) may be mixed in different ratios to accommodate both paper and film. The hypo (fix) may also be used for a number of rolls of film.

HYPO NEUTRALIZER

Hypo neutralizer is a solution which enables the washing time to be reduced. Negatives which have been washed for a few minutes may be transferred to the hypo neutralizer and then washed for a specified time. The total washing time may be shortened, which is a serious consideration when a warm water supply is limited.

WASH

The wash removes the hypo. The film remains, including the blackened particles of silver which make up the photographic image.

WETTING AGENT (PHOTO-FLO, an Eastman Kodak product)

The wetting agent is important in that it helps the film to dry without water marks. Water marks are usually permanent, and cause marks to appear on the print. Wetting agents are highly concentrated and must be diluted for use. A prepared solution accommodates many rolls of film.

FILM-DEVELOPING PROCEDURE

The following is the necessary equipment for developing roll film.

1. Chemicals needed to develop film.

>   Developer
>   Developer Replinisher, if used.
>   Stop Bath
>   Hypo (fix)
>   Hypo Neutralizer, if used.
>   Wetting Agent

2. Containers (bottles) for the above solutions.

3. Film Developing Tank (Ansco-matic or Nikor)

4. Thermometer

5. Timer

6. Viscose Sponge or Sterile Cotton

7. Film Clips (pinch type clothes pins)

The following is a basic procedure for developing roll film. It may be altered, depending on the particular facilities available.

LOAD FILM ON REEL

The film is sensitive to all colors of light which necessitates loading it onto the reel *in total darkness*. The lid of the developing tank must be sucured before turning on the lights.

OBTAIN CHEMICALS

Be certain that there is enough solution to fill the developing tank. Otherwise, part of the negative might be underdeveloped. Have beakers with all the necessary chemicals at your disposal before starting. There should be a minimum amount of time lost in changing from one solution to another.

CHECK DEVELOPER FOR CONTAMINATION (If chemicals are available for general use)

Insert litmus paper into the developer. Watch the color change. *Kelly green* - no contamination. *Orange* - DO NOT USE.

CHECK TEMPERATURE OF CHEMICALS

The temperature range is 68° - 75°F. Warm or cool the solution if it is necessary. Consult the Developer Time - Temperature Chart for the developing time. The time varies with the temperature.

POUR IN DEVELOPER

Agitate for the first 30 seconds, 5 seconds every 30 seconds thereafter for the remaining time.

DRAIN DEVELOPER

If a developer-replenisher is used, add the replenisher to the developer storage bottle before pouring the developer back into it. If there is to be an overflow, it is better to have used developer overflow.

WATER RINSE or STOP BATH

The temperature range is again 68° - 75°F. Fill the developing tank with running water, agitate it, and then empty it. Repeat this twice. If a stop bath is used, fill the tank, agitate it for 10 seconds, and then empty it.

POUR IN HYPO (FIX)

The temperature range is again 68° - 75°F. Agitate periodically. After 3 minutes, the lid may be removed. The total time in the hypo (fix) is dependent upon the brand used. Do not remove the film from the reel unless it is on a Nikor developing reel. The Nikor reels enable wet film to be reloaded. The plastic reels do not.

DRAIN HYPO (FIX)

The hypo (fix) is reusable. Pour the solution back into its container.

FINAL RINSE

The temperature range is 68° - 75°F. Rinse for 20 minutes, with rapid changes of water. Empty the tank periodically.

SOAK IN WETTING AGENT

The temperature range is 68° - 75°F. Soak the film in the wetting agent, for example Eastman Kodak Photo-Flo, for no longer than 30 seconds. A prepared solution may be used for many rolls of film.

REMOVE FILM FROM DEVELOPING REEL

Attach film to a hanging negative clip. Wipe both sides with a sponge or cotton moistened with a wetting agent.

DRYING THE FILM

The film should dry in a dust-free area. A negative clip should be attached to the bottom of the film in order to help prevent it from curling.

UNSHARP NEGATIVES

The sharpness of photographs is basically dependent upon the quality of the camera's lens. An expensive camera will have a sharper lens than an inexpensive one. In fact, the lenses on most inexpensive cameras are now made of plastic, and will never really produce an extremely sharp image. However, there are other causes for unsharpness, beyond the limitations of a lens.

1. MOTION OF CAMERA

The most common cause for unsharp photographs is the movement of the photographer during the exposure. To prevent this movement the photographer must stand still, hold his breath, and then gently press the shutter release. A shutter speed below 1/30 of a second should not be used when hand holding a camera. A tripod or improvised support should be used for slow shutter speeds.

2. MOTION OF THE SUBJECT

Motion of the subject results from a failure to use a shutter speed fast enough to adequately stop the motion of the subject. The speed of the subject, and the angle at which the subject approaches the camera are variables to be considered.

3. IMPROPER FOCUS

The photographer focuses on the wrong object in a scene and the principle object may be partially or way out of focus. Focusing is especially critical in dark situations when a large aperture is required.

4. LACK OF SUFFICIENT DEPTH OF FIELD

The amount of depth of field depends on the size of the aperture. In dark situations, depth of field must be sacrificed in order to obtain sufficient exposure. In other situations, a slower shutter speed may be permissible, enabling one to obtain more depth of field. For example, a shutter speed of 1/500 of a second is not required for the exposure of a landscape. By using a slower shutter speed, a different F/Number may be used. Because of the smaller aperture, more depth of field is possible.

5. DIRT ON THE LENS

Dirt, dust, and particularly fingerprints reduce the effective sharpness of a lens. The lens must be kept clean.

6. ATMOSPHERIC AND HEAT HAZE

The atmospheric haze in a landscape is usually visible and may be partially corrected with filters. Heat haze is not as easily seen or eliminated. However, heat haze is not common in most areas.

CARE OF NEGATIVES

A negative is delicate. It is easily wrinkled and highly susceptible to scratches. A scratch appears as a black mark on the photograph and is permanent. Retouching of the negative is usually too difficult with the small negative from roll film cameras. Dirt or lint may be brushed or blown off a negative before it is printed, but a fingerprint is not easily removed. Wiping the fingerprint may scratch the film. A wad of cotton moistened with *carbon tetrachloride* or pure alcohol will help remove them. The answer is not to have fingerprints on the negatives at all. Handle the film only by its edges.

The negative should be respected as part of the esthetic experience. The negative produces the photograph. The imagery of a photograph is neglected by the observer if poor quality is dominant. After the negatives have dried, they should be removed from the drying area. The longer they are left, the greater the danger of the adherence of dust and dirt.

The film should be cut into strips approximately six inches long. One should never cut each negative individually, as they would be much too hard to handle. The short strips should be stored in envelopes (available for all film sizes at photographic supply stores) or wrapped in folded paper. It is necessary to keep negatives in a clean dry place.

PRINTING

Photographs are made by passing light through a negative onto a light sensitive paper. The negative, opposite in tone from the original scene, projects an image onto the paper which, upon exposure and development, produces a positive print. The black areas on a negative produce white on a photograph because the black areas prevent light from passing. Where a negative is clear (transparent), the photograph will be black, and the medium toned areas on a negative will produce medium toned areas on the photograph.

Negative.

Positive print.

The light sensitive paper is basically the same as film, the major difference being the support. The film emulsion is on acetate, a transparent material. The paper emulsion is on paper.

The paper emulsions are not as fast as film, nor are they panchromatic (sensitive to all colors). Photographic paper is purposely made insensitive to yellow light. The printing darkrooms have yellow safelights providing enough illumination for one to print, while not affecting the paper.

The tone, surface and speed of photographic paper may be confusing. The market is flooded with different types and brands. Beginning students have the tendency to switch from one type to another in the hope of trying them all. This is based on excitement, not dissatisfaction. This practice is not recommended because it is best to understand fully one brand and type before considering another.

The following are aspects to be considered when describing or analyzing the qualities of photographic paper:

Tone   Thickness
Surface   Contrast
Speed

TONE

Some papers have a warm tone, whereas others have a cold tone. A paper whose tones are brownish (a brown-black) is a warm tone paper. A cold tone paper is one in which the tones are primarily a blue-black.

SURFACE

Photographic paper is available with different surfaces. Some of these surfaces resemble burlap, linen or silk, while others have a dull mat surface. The pros and cons about the use of textured paper are controversial. Some schools of thought endorse the use of these textured papers, while others are fervently against their use.

SPEED

The speed of photographic papers varies. Some papers are more sensitive to light than others. There are basically two classifications:

1. Contact Printing Paper
2. Projection Printing Paper

The contact printing paper is considerably slower than enlarging or projection paper because the light source is closer to the paper than when enlarging.

THICKNESS

Photographic papers are available in two thicknesses, *single weight* and *double weight*. The thickness of double weight paper is twice that of the single weight. Single weight paper is most commonly used because it is cheaper. Double weight paper is recommended for large enlargements (11" x 14" or 16" x 20"), because it has less tendency to wrinkle.

CONTRAST

Present day films have enough latitude for exposure in a wide variety of lighting situations to produce printable negatives. A negative exposed on a bright sunny day would tend to be contrasty, that is, it would have deep dark shadows with very bright highlights. A negative exposed on a cloudy day would be flat, with little contrast, due to the overall level of illumination.

The original method of printing negatives was contact printing. Gradually, as optics and materials improved, enlarging became practical. At present the following two methods are being used.

1. Contact Printing
2. Projection Printing - Enlarging

1. CONTACT PRINTING

Contact printing is the original method of printing, and is still used today when the maximum degree of quality is desired. Contact printing consists of putting photographic paper on top of the negative (held flat with glass) and exposing it to light. The emulsion side of the negative, which is dull, must be the side which is in contact with the shiny side of the paper. The dull side is the emulsion for film, while the shiny side is the emulsion for paper.

> Film - Emulsion side is dull
> Paper - Emulsion side is shiny

The type of photographic paper used for contact printing depends upon the method of exposure. Generally, contact printing paper is used, but the following methods enable the use of enlarging paper. These methods simplify the amount and variety of paper the photographer must keep in storage.

The simplest method of contact printing involves the use of a piece of plate glass (free from scratches) and a bare light bulb. The enlarging paper is placed on a table (emulsion side up), the negative is placed on top (emulsion side down), and both are sandwiched together by the glass. The light bulb is turned on and off for the exposure.

The second method involves the use of a *contact printing frame*. A contact printing frame is a wooden or metal frame having a spring back which holds the negative and paper together under the glass. The enlarging or contact printing paper in the contact printing frame may be exposed by either the light from a bulb hanging from the ceiling or by the projected beam of light from an enlarger. Because of its aperture, the use of the enlarger as a light source allows for more control in exposure.

The *contact printer* is a device which has a self-contained light source. See the following illustration.

Contact printing frame.

Contact printer

Because the light source is so close to the negative and photographic paper, a paper with a slow speed is usually necessary. This paper is *contact printing paper*. Because it is considerably slower than enlarging paper, contact printing paper may not be overexposed as easily as enlarging paper. However, many contact printers may be modified in order that enlarging paper may be used. A bulb of lower wattage than normal need only be substituted.

Using the contact printer, the negative is laid on the glass (dull or emulsion side up), and the photographic paper is placed on top (emulsion or shiny side down). The lid which keeps the negative and paper in firm contact is then pulled down on top of them. Many contact printers have catch mechanisms which lock the lid down. A switch turns the light on and off for exposure.

Many contact printers have more than one bulb for exposure. They sometimes have a whole series of tiny bulbs which may be turned off or on independently. As a result, local areas may be made lighter or darker. It is the contact printing method of dodging.

PROOF SHEETS

A proof sheet is a contact print which includes all of the negatives from a single roll of film. It is made in the same manner as a contact print. Consult the section entitled contact printing for complete details.

The use of proof sheets is recommended because the proof sheet roughly shows what the finished print will look like. By examining a proof sheet, one is able to have an idea of the imagery and of whether or not his negatives are properly exposed and in focus.

If a number of different exposures are made of one subject, proof sheets allow one to make a selection. Proof sheets are also a system for organizing negatives. Each proof sheet has a number corresponding to a particular group of negatives. It is better to handle proof sheets when searching for a negative than it is to handle the negative itself. Negatives on the same roll of film have different densities. As a result, some portions of the proof sheet are lighter than others. Pieces of opaque paper, the same width as the negatives, may be used to give the denser negatives more exposure, thus evening out the basic exposure of the proof sheet.

72

2. ENLARGING

Historically speaking, the process of enlarging is a rather recent development. Contact printing, which produces prints the same size as the negative, was the first method of printing used. This method necessitates the use of large bulky cameras. However, as enlarging equipment improved, more practical printing became possible. Today, with the quality and precision of optics in both the camera and the enlarger, prints of good quality may be obtained from rather small negatives. As a result, the size of cameras has been greatly reduced.

The enlarger is basically a camera in reverse. Instead of absorbing light, the enlarger projects it. A developed negative takes the place of the light sensitive film. Light is passed through the negative in the enlarger, and is focused on the easel. The enlarger, by increasing or decreasing the distance between the lens and the easel, allows the size of the projected image to be changed. There are many brands of enlargers on the market. However, they are all basically of two types:
1. Condenser
2. Diffusion

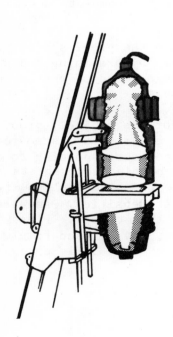

Condenser enlarger.

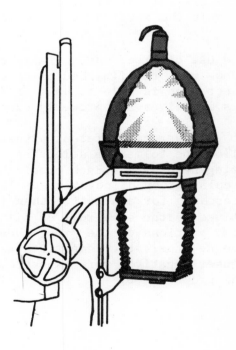

Diffusion enlarger.

1. THE CONDENSER ENLARGER

The condenser enlarger uses lenses (condensers) for concentrating light
and projects a very sharp, clearly defined image. An enlargement made
with a condenser enlarger is sharper than that made with a diffusion
enlarger.

2. THE DIFFUSION ENLARGER

The diffusion enlarger slightly diffuses the projected image which
minimizes the presence of scratches, dust and dirt on the negative.
It is often used for commercial purposes. Generally, a diffusion
enlarger is not recommended, as enough image quality is lost due to
enlarging without purposely destroying it. The selection of an enlarger is an important consideration. It is necessary to consider present
and anticipated needs. The enlarger should match the quality of the
camera. For instance, it would be very foolish to use a poor quality
enlarger with negatives from a camera of very good quality. The resulting photographs would leave much to be desired.

In printing, the emulsion side of the negative must always face the
emulsion side of the paper. Otherwise, the subject of the photograph
is backwards. In such a case, words appear backwards.

The enlarger has three adjustments; the size, the sharpness, and the
relative brightness of the projected image. Size is determined by the
distance between the negative and the easel. The further the negative
from the easel, the larger the projected image. Any changes in magnification must be accompanied by focusing. If they are not, the projected image will be out of focus. Brightness is determined by the
aperture (the F/Number), which is operated in the same manner on the
enlarger as it is on the camera. Before exposure, the aperture should
be closed down to at least two F/Numbers from the maximum opening.
The use of a small aperture insures sharp focus. As the aperture is
opened or closed from one F/Number to another, the stops may be felt
with the fingers. This is an advantage in the subdued light of a
printing darkroom.

TONAL QUALITY

Photography, a graphic process, is a consideration of values and how
they relate to each other. The original scene, when photographed
and printed, is rendered in respective values ranging from pure white
through a wide range of grays to black.

The manipulation of these tones is a technical skill. A photograph
must be printed correctly in order for it to have the desired visual
quality. However, printing is more than a technical accomplishment.
It is an esthetic process. Printing enables the photographer to state
his ideas visually.

Beginning photographers are often so intrigued with the photographic
process that they neglect to consider technique. Any print, regardless
of its quality, seems to look good. It is magic to see the image appear from a blank piece of paper during development. However, the
quality of a good photograph requires a more sophisticated attitude.
Is it too light? Is it too dark? Is it too flat? Is it too contrasty?
These are questions that are not answered verbally. Decisions must be
made by visually analyzing the tones of the photograph.

The prints of beginning photographers are often flat, having a monotone
of light grays. The negative is normal, but the print lacks contrast
because they fail to see a really rich black. In order to see correctly what a black is, a sample may be made. Expose a small piece of
photographic paper, develop it for two minutes, transfer it to the
stop bath, and upon completion in the hypo, examine it. Repeat the
steps until the best possible black is obtained. Wash and dry this
sample in order that it may be compared to other blacks in succeeding
photographs. The comparison of a real black to a suspected black graph-
ically shows the difference. Once a real black is seen, and the difference observed between a dull black and a rich black, the tonal qualities
of the photograph improve.

EXPOSURE

The first consideration in printing is the overall exposure of the photograph. How dark should the photograph be? Again, this may only be determined visually. Compare the visual quality of the following three photographs.

All three photographs are from the same negative, and printed on the same contrast paper. The exposure is the only variable. The first print is an accurate, realistic rendition of the house and surroundings. It has the quality which a real estate broker would find useful in selling the house. The second print is slightly darker because of a longer exposure, and has a different visual quality. The shadows are darker, the clouds are more defined, and the house is more pronounced. It has a moody quality which the first print lacks. The visual quality of the third print is more extreme than that of the second, and perhaps the opposite of the first. The photograph no longer appears to be pleasant. In fact, it is rather hostile or spooky. This type of photograph would never be used by a real estate agent unless he were attempting to sell the house to a very specific type of clientele. With the above three photographs it is evident that the quality of imagery is influenced by the exposure. In some situations, an exaggeration is good, whereas in others it is not. Again, the proper amount of exposure may only be determined visually. Because photographic paper is expensive, it is best to use *test strips* to determine the general exposure.

TEST STRIPS

A test strip for an 8" x 10" print is a sheet of photographic paper which is cut into strips (roughly 2" x 10"), and used as a test to evaluate the contrast and exposure of the photograph. The use of very small test strips (smaller than suggested) is more economical, but usually unsatisfactory. It is difficult to make the necessary evaluations because only a small amount of the print may be seen. The placement of the test strip is also important. A test strip should be placed diagonally across the print, or across the most important part of the projected image on the easel.

Contrast and exposure may be estimated during enlarging by observing how the negative appears as it is projected on the easel. If the image is very bright, it requires less exposure than if it is very dark. With practice it is easier to estimate the initial exposure and contrast for the test strip. A series of five second exposures is a point of departure. In doing this, expose the entire test strip for 5 seconds, then cover 3/4 of it and expose again. Repeat this with the test strip 1/2 covered, and again with only 1/4 covered. The test strip will have four different exposures. The paper which is used for covering during the exposure must be opaque. Be careful not to move the test strip during the process. If the longest exposure is too light, repeat the operation with longer exposures. If it is too dark, repeat with shorter exposures.

#3 contrast paper at five second intervals.

#3 contrast paper at two second intervals.

#3 contrast paper at one second intervals.

The exposure for all finished prints should be roughly 15 to 20 seconds. A one or two second exposure will not allow for any manipulations such as burning-in or dodging. If it is necessary, close the diaphragm (aperture) down farther to lengthen the exposure. Exposures longer than 40 seconds may cause the negative to swell because of the heat. When this happens, the film buckles and causes the image to be out of focus. A glass negative carrier prevents this from happening.

The test strip is developed and processed in a normal manner. Consistency is essential. If the test strip is developed for two minutes, the final print is also developed for two minutes. The use of test strips is an economical manner of determining the visual quality of a photograph.

CONTRAST

The second consideration in printing is contrast. How do the blacks and whites relate? Is there a great difference between them, or are they rather a monotone?

The contrast of a negative is determined by its exposure and development. If every negative were perfectly exposed and developed, printing would be easier. However, in practice negatives appear which have a different contrast range than those normally exposed and developed. See the following illustrations.

Normal negative.

Contrasty negative.

Flat negative.

A photographic paper which would produce a good print from a normally exposed and developed negative would not produce a good print from a contrasty or flat negative. As a result, photographic paper is made in a number of different contrasts, in order to compensate for the different types of negatives. If a negative is contrasty, a paper which is flat is used, in order to balance out the extreme range of tones. Similarly, a flat negative requires a contrasty paper. The paper is numbered 1 - 4, indicating different degrees of contrast. #1 paper is flat and is used for contrasty negatives. #4 paper is contrasty and is used for flat negatives.

        #1 contrast paper is for contrasty negatives
        #2 contrast paper is for normal negatives
        #3 contrast paper is for slightly flat negatives
        #4 contrast paper is for flat negatives

There is another type of paper (variable contrast paper) which allows for different ranges of contrast through filtration. Consult the appendix for the section entitled "Variable Contrast Paper."

The ability of photography to record a scene with a full range of gray tones is one of its inherent qualities. It is important for the photographer to take full advantage of this tonal range. Perfect exposure and correct development are essential. Any deviation results in an exaggeration of contrast. However, in some situations the exposure and development may be altered in order to change the effective contrast of a scene. The contrast of the scene may be reduced or increased in order that the resulting negative may print on #2 paper. A technique called *overexposure and underdevelopment* or *underexposure and overdevelopment* is used to achieve this end. Consult the appendix.

Ideally, in order to achieve the maximum number of tones, a negative should be printed on number two paper which produces an ample range of tone, and yet is versatile. However, it is possible to have a great variety in contrast by using the other papers.

#6 contrast paper at three second intervals.

#3 contrast paper at two second intervals.

#1 contrast paper at one second intervals.

Final photograph.

The beginning photographer often confuses contrast with exposure. Often after examining a test strip and seeing that it is too light he changes contrast. He has confused exposure with contrast. If a test strip is too light, make it darker and then decide whether a change in contrast is necessary. Deal with one variable at a time. With experience, the two variables may be handled together. Decisions then come naturally.

Sometimes one quality seems correct but the other does not. Printing is the consideration of both of these qualities - exposure and contrast. They cannot be separated. It is the relationship between them which produces the desired tones in a photograph.

The selection of exposure and contrast combinations is a technical decision. Even more important, it is an esthetic decision. It is the consideration, evaluation and relation of these tones which enables the photographer to state his ideas visually.

Compare the visual quality of the following three prints. All of them were made from the same normal negative. Only the contrast differs.

The first print has a stark white and black appearance. It is too contrasty. The skin tone is too white and contains no detail. In this particular situation, an excess of contrast is detrimental to the subject. The second print is the most realistic condition. The tones are rich, and yet have some detail. The third print is a monotone; the blacks are not rich and the whites have a gray appearance. The photograph is too flat. The skin tone is too dark. It makes the boy appear older than he is. In adult male portraiture, this quality is sometimes desirable, in order to help convey the idea of ruggedness. The relative tone of skin is related to preconceived ideas of how the tones should appear. Usually, a light, soft quality is desired, in preference to a dark, somber tonality.

In comparing the prints (contrasty and flat) in the following example, it may be difficult to judge which tonality is best. There is no norm in this case as there is when printing a skin tone. Some may feel that the print with more contrast is better while others may feel that the flat print is best. Here there is room for a greater range of opinion. It depends upon the message of the photograph. If it is to be considered a non-objective form, a deviation from the norm may be beneficial. In this case, either the flat or the contrasty photograph may be the best. The subject must be considered in relation to the respective range of tones. A non-objective subject usually allows for the greatest degree of deviation.

Often a negative is made which is very light. A faint image may be
visible, but a print may not be possible. A negative needs an ample
tonal range with sufficient density in order to yield a satisfactory
print. Sometimes a technique called *intensification* may save an underexposed or underdeveloped negative. Consult the section on "Intensification and Reduction" in the appendix.

The opposite condition involves a negative which is basically opaque,
a negative which is overexposed and/or overdeveloped. In this case,
a technique called *reduction* may salvage the negative. Consult the
appendix for complete details.

Film is capable of recording more tones than may be printed; in fact,
the paper may record only one third of the tones possible on the negative. As a result, detail may be visible in the negative, but may appear as black in the photograph. This may often be corrected through
local manipulations. Often a print has a small area which is either too
dark or too light. The overall appearance of the print may be satisfactory, with the exception of this area. By *dodging* or *burning-in,*
this area of the print may be lightened or darkened

      Dodging - Lightens areas of a photograph
      Burning-in - Darkens areas of a photograph

DODGING

Dodging lightens areas of a photograph by obstructing some of the light during the exposure. This obstruction causes that specific area to receive less light. Pieces of black paper, varying in size and shape, are fastened on wire and are used as dodgers. These dodgers must be kept in constant motion and far enough above the easel so that the dodged area blends with the rest of the print. Otherwise a line will be noticeable. The length of time of the dodging and the size of the dodger are determined by tests.

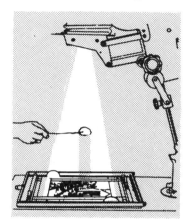

Dodging.

Uncorrected.

Corrected.

BURNING-IN

Burning-in is the opposite of dodging. It consists of bringing out detail in a negative which normally wouldn't be seen. This detail would appear too light in the resulting print. The technique of burning-in includes exposing the photograph in a normal manner, then, without moving the photograph, re-exposing the area to be darkened.

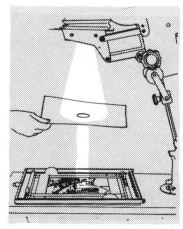

Burning-in.

Uncorrected.

Corrected.

ENLARGING - PROCEDURE

Although enlargers vary in their manner of operation, the following
is the basic procedure in making an enlarged print.

1. CHECK THE FOCAL LENGTH OF THE ENLARGING LENS

Check to see that the lens on the enlarger is the correct size for the
film to be used. An enlarging lens for a small film size will not adequately cover the area of a large negative. A lens for a large negative generally does not permit enough magnification when used with
small film.

2. PLACE THE NEGATIVE IN A CARRIER

The emulsion side (dull side) of the negative should be face down,
towards the lens. If it is not, everything is backwards in the print.
The negative carrier must be the right size for the negative. A small
negative in a large carrier allows light to spill around its borders,
which fogs paper during the exposure. Other enlargers, whose carriers
hold the negatives between glass, require masking off the clear glass
area. Some enlargers even have a masking device which is built in.

3. CLEAN THE NEGATIVE

Remove all lint and dust. Camel hair brushes or compressed air are
suggested. It is necessary always to handle negatives by their edges
in order to avoid marring their surfaces with fingerprints.

4. PLACE THE NEGATIVE CARRIER IN THE ENLARGER

The condenser or lamp housing is lifted, and the negative carrier is inserted. When working in a group situation, one should never have the enlarger light on when inserting or removing the negative carrier. The
stray light fogs (exposes) other people's paper.

5. PLACE A WHITE SHEET OF PAPER IN THE PRINT EASEL

The paper provides a surface on which to see the projected image. Some easels have a white surface, making the use of white paper unnecessary.

6. TURN THE ENLARGER LIGHT ON

First, the aperture of the lens is opened as wide as possible. The size of the print is then decided upon, and the enlarger raised or lowered accordingly. The focus must be adjusted each time the enlarger is raised or lowered. After this, the aperture is closed down at least two stops or clicks.

7. EXPOSE THE TEST STRIP

It is a good practice to first check that the aperture is closed down. The projected image may be examined to determine what contrast paper is necessary. If the image looks contrasty, it is wise to begin with #2 paper. If it appears to be flat, #4 paper may be used at first. The enlarger light is then turned off and a test strip inserted into the easel.

8. DEVELOP THE TEST STRIP

The test strip is developed in the same manner as any other print is developed. If the test strip appears too dark on the whole, it has been overexposed. In this case, the aperture must be closed down another stop (a total of 3 clicks), and another test strip made. If the test strip appears too light, another test strip must be made using 10 second exposures. An extremely dark negative may require 20 second exposures, or longer.

9. EXPOSE THE FULL SHEET

The previous test indicated what exposure produces the best photograph. A full sheet of paper is placed in the easel and exposed accordingly. This print should be successful.

Because of the many variables (the density of each negative, the state of the chemicals, the difference between one enlarger and another, and the difference in magnification of the image), it is necessary to make many test strips. Even when reprinting a negative, the test strip is necessary.

DEVELOPMENT PROCEDURE

The development of printing paper is basically the same as that of film.
There is a developer, a stop bath (a means of stopping the reaction),
and the hypo (fix). The method of handling prints is slightly different,
as are the immersion times. Processing is done in trays arranged in a
row.

Chemicals are mixed before use and stored in concentrated form. Their
dilution with water depends on the individual solution, the particular
brand of chemical, and the desired tonality. The following is a list
of chemicals necessary for printing.

> Developer
> Stop Bath
> Hypo (fix)
> Hypo Neutralizer, if desired

The chemicals may irritate one's hands and cause a rash. The developer
tends to stain finger nails brown. Print tongs are suggested in order
that one's hands do not come in contact with the chemicals. It is important not to contaminate the solutions with the tongs by placing a
tong from one solution into another. The tong which is in the developer remains there.

On evaporation, some chemicals leave a residue. Hypo leaves a white
scum. The developer will stain clothing and looks as if coffee were
spilled. None of the chemicals are poisonous. The acids used are
so diluted that there is no danger of burns. None are explosive. If
used properly, all of the chemicals are harmless.

DEVELOPER

The developer brings out the image. It is imperative that one agitate
the solution while this is happening. After twenty seconds the image
should slowly begin to appear. The print must be developed *one to two
minutes* in order for it to have the proper tonal range. A common mistake is to overexpose the print and develop it for less than a minute.
In such a case, the print is mottled and does not have a good range of
tones. Another mistake is to develop beyond the two minutes. In this
case, the print may stain. If, after two minute development, the print
is still too light, it requires more exposure.

There are many brands of paper developers on the market. Dektol, an
Eastman Kodak product, has been a standard and commonly used paper
developer for many years. It is well suited for situations such as
schools, where large quantities are required, as well as for individual use.

STOP BATH

The stop bath is a diluted acetic acid solution which neutralizes the
developer. It is usually available in a 28% concentrate solution and
is diluted for use in the proportion of 1 1/2 oz. per 32 oz. water.
After the print has developed for two minutes, it is drained briefly
and then placed in the stop bath for 10 - 15 seconds. Running water is
sometimes used in place of the acetic acid solution, but it is not as
effective.

HYPO (FIX)

The silver particles exposed during the enlargement turn black in the
developer. Other silver particles which were not exposed must be removed. Hypo is literally a collector of undeveloped silver particles.
If these silver particles were not removed, they would eventually turn
black, destroying the permanence of the image.

If a large number of prints is to be processed, the use of two hypo
trays is recommended. Hypo in the first tray is exhausted before that
in the second tray. As a result, the first solution is periodically
checked for exhaustion. There are a number of products available for
this purpose. When it is found to be exhausted, it is discarded and
the second tray of solution moved into its place. Fresh hypo is then
put in the place of the second hypo. The use of two hypo trays allows for the processing of a large number of prints in a given amount
of solution.

The print should be drained briefly before it is placed in the hypo
(fix), where it should remain for about three minutes. It should then
be transferred to the second hypo for another five minutes, a total
of eight minutes. These times apply to Kodak Rapid Fix and may vary
with other brands. It is important to agitate the print periodically.
After two minutes in the first hypo, the print may be inspected in
normal light.

The manner of examining the print in the light varies, depending on
the available facilities. The print may either be placed in a tray
and carried into a normally lighted room, or left in the tray and the
light turned on. Generally speaking, in a classroom situation, the
print must be carried into another room for inspection. Using an
8" x 10" tray for this purpose prevents hypo from dripping from the
print onto the floor or other subjects.

When examining the print in normal room light, one must decide whether
the contrast is correct and whether the print is too dark or too light.
One must also decide if the imagery of the photograph is worthwhile.
This is the time when the quality of the photograph must be evaluated.
It is important always to judge the photograph in normal room light,
never in the darkroom under the yellow safelight.

WASH

Photographs must be washed for an hour with rapid changes of water.
The temperature of the water must never be lower than 65°F. or higher
than 80°F. In certain areas, a large supply of warm water is a problem in the winter. The use of a hypo neutralizer helps to conserve
water. Consult the section concerning hypo neutralizer (on page 63)
for further information.

The temperature for the solutions for photographic paper development
is not as critical as that of film. Room temperature (68° - 75°F.)
is satisfactory. The wash water should never be colder than 65°F. or
hotter than 80°F.

DRYING

The manner of drying prints depends on the facilities available.
Cheap electric driers are usually unsatisfactory as they do not dry
the prints evenly, and the edges generally curl. In schools or commercial situations, the large drum type driers are needed in order to
handle the large volume of prints. A simple method for drying a limited number of prints involves placing washed prints between photographic
blotters. Desk blotters are not used because they contain lint which
sticks to the surface of the prints.

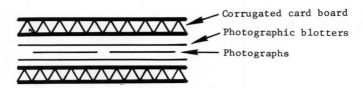

Corrugated card board
Photographic blotters
Photographs

The corrugated cardboard is important. It allows for free circulation
of air, and prevents the mass of wet blotters from adhering together.
Even though it takes a few days for the prints to dry, they are flat.
Weights (books) should be placed on the pile to keep it compressed.

BLOTTER ROLLS, BLOTTER BOOKS

The use of a *blotter roll* is also suggested as a means of drying prints.
Eastman Kodak provides a large and small size. The blotter roll is
based on the principle described above. However, the wet prints are
rolled instead of laid flat. *Blotter books* are also available. However, their capacity for holding prints is usually too limited to be
really practical.

SCREENS

Some photographers lay their prints face down on plastic window screen-
ing which has been stretched across a frame. The back side of the print
is covered with a photographic blotter which helps to keep the prints
from curling.

HANGING WET PRINTS

One of the simplest methods of drying prints is to merely hang them
from a taut line in the same manner as clothing. The excess water is
wiped off and the prints are hung back to back with pinch type cloths
pins. Two pins are also fastened to the bottom.

DRY MOUNTING

A photograph is difficult to keep flat. A curled print is hard to look
at and the surface of the print (the emulsion) may crack as one attempts
to flatten it. A photograph mounted on a pliable surface, such as a
thin piece of mount board, solves this problem. An attempt to glue or
paste a photograph to the mount board is not satifactory. Glues and
pastes, as well as being messy, may stain the photograph. The correct
material to use is *dry mount tissue*. Dry mount tissue becomes tacky
when heated and will adhere the photograph to the mount board. Dry
mounting is dry, neat, permanent, and easily done.

Some brands of dry mount tissue have sheets of paper separating each
piece of tissue. Eastman Kodak uses a pink sheet. It is important
not to confuse the pink sheet with the tissue. The pink sheet is only
used for separation.

A sheet of dry mount tissue may be tacked to the back of the photograph
in the center with a *tacking iron*. The white borders must be trimmed
with the dry mount tissue tacked to the back of the photograph. It is
important that none of the dry mount tissue extends beyond the photograph after the trimming. If this occurs, the photograph will later
stick to the heated *dry mount press*. The trimmed photograph must then
be placed on the mount board and spaced.

Dry mount press.   Tacking iron.

The manner or style of placing a photograph varies. Some people prefer
"bleed mounting," whereas others prefer a more classical manner. Bleed
mounting consists of trimming the mount board flush with the print. The
resulting mounted photograph has no white border. The classical manner
involves mounting the print on white mount board with white borders.

After the photograph is spaced on the mount board, a corner of the photograph is carefully lifted and the dry mount tissue is tacked to the board. Because the tacking iron will damage the emulsion, it should never touch the surface of the photograph. At this point, the photograph is ready to be inserted in the dry mount press. It is very important to have the photograph covered with a piece of paper before closing the press. The photograph must never touch the metal of the dry mount press. After 30 seconds in the closed press, the photograph must be removed. It will be permanently adhered to the mount board.

Attempting to dry mount with a clothing iron is not recommended. This procedure may be satisfactory for small prints (4" x 5" or smaller) but not very satisfactory for larger ones. Heat must be applied to the entire area of the print at once. It cannot be a piecemeal application.

The dial on the iron should be set between silk and wool. The surface of the iron must be thoroughly cleaned after use, as shellac from the dry mount tissue adheres to the surface of the iron and is easily transferred onto clothing.

SPOTTING

1. WHITE SPOTS

The surface of the finished print often includes tiny areas of white which are called spots. They may be the result of fingerprints, scratches on the backing of the film, or tiny dust and dirt particles which settle either on the negative or the print surface. Because these substances are opaque, they prevent the light from exposing the paper. Dust particles are sometimes too small to be readily seen on the negative, yet they appear on the print.

Spots are especially noticeable after a print has been dried and mounted. At this time, the technique of spotting is used. Spotting is the application of a blend of a black dye (Spotone) and water to the white area or spot on the finished print. Materials needed for spotting include Spotone, a 000 brush, a palette for mixing, and a container for water. Spotone is available in three different colors depending on whether the photographic paper is warm or cool toned. Number 3 is required for cool tone paper. Various dilutions of number 1 and number 2 are used for warm toned papers. In practice, the dye is applied dot by dot with a small brush. That is, tiny brush tips of dye are applied to the white area or spot until the value of that area approximates the value of the surrounding areas with a number of applications.

The secret of effective spotting includes the careful application of Spotone. It also includes avoiding making several common mistakes. The first of these involves making the spotted area darker in value than the surrounding area. It is well to remember that Spotone does not wash off after it has been applied to the surface of a print. Another mistake occurs when the beginner attempts to spot in a manner used for water color painting. He may attempt to use brush strokes rather than dots. Such an attempt makes it extremely difficult to keep the dye within the confines of the white area. If the dye overlaps the surrounding areas, the imperfection is even more noticeable. There may also be too much moisture on the brush. In such a case, the brush deposits a drop of Spotone considerably larger than the area to be spotted. This, again, is more noticeable than the original white spot.

2. BLACK SPOTS

A black spot which appears on a print results from a clear, transparent area on the negative. The two common causes are scratches and air bubbles present on the film during development.

The attempt to spot the negative with Spotone or opaque (a paint which adheres to film surfaces and is used to block out areas) is usually impossible because of the small size of the negative. However, the print may be spotted as a remedy. The technique is slightly more complicated than that used for spotting a white area on the print. The black areas are bleached with a concentrated solution of potassium ferricyonide or with ordinary laundry bleach (for example Clorox). A toothpick with cotton wrapped around its point is dipped into the bleach and then carefully applied to the spot. With a few applications the black spot will turn white. This white spot can then be spotted in the normal manner.

Spotting is the final operation in the presentation of a photograph, and should not be neglected. A photograph, regardless of its quality of imagery, has a poor appearance of it is covered with white or black spots.

APPENDIX   I

AVAILABLE LIGHT	SHEET FILM
CLOSE-UPS	STROBE - ELECTRONIC FLASH,
COMPENSATING DEVELOPERS	FLASH BULBS
COPYING	THIN EMULSION FILMS
EXPOSING COLOR FILM	THREE DIMENSION-STEREO
DEVELOPING FILM BY INSPECTION	TONING
FILM PACK	TWO-BATH DEVELOPER
FILTERS	UNDER-OVER FILM DEVELOPING
FINE GRAIN	VARIABLE CONTRAST PAPER
INTENSIFICATION AND REDUCTION	VIEW CAMERA MOVEMENTS
MONO-BATH DEVELOPERS	WEIGHT AND TEMPERATURE-
POLAROID	CONVERSION CHART

AVAILABLE LIGHT

The advent of the small miniature camera, which possesses a fast lens and uses fast film, allows photographs to be made without supplementary light (flash bulbs or strobe). The use of available light provides a more realistic quality, as the original lighting of the situation is more faithfully rendered. The subjects are also not as aware of the camera and, as a result, are more relaxed, normal and unposed.

The following three considerations must be taken into account when using available light:

    1. The lens on the camera
    2. The film speed (A.S.A.)
    3. The film developer

The camera needs a lens which has a maximum F/Number of at least F/2. A fast film such as Eastman Kodak's Tri-X or Ansco Super Hypan is needed. Fast film requires a high energy developer such as U.F.G. or Acufine in order to obtain maximum film speed. The film speed (A.S.A.) is a function of the film developer used. Some developers are able to increase the relative film speed (A.S.A.) by a factor of twice and often four times that of the normal film speed.

In available light photography the lighting is often very contrasty and requires a careful meter reading. A lens hood is a necessary item in order to help prevent glare. Frequently there are people in the scene, making it necessary to take a meter reading off a skin tone. If it is too dark for this reading, a white card may be used as a substitute for the skin tone. A correct reading is approximately 2 1/2 times the exposure indicated from the white card. It is important not to overexpose the negatives. Available light photographs, because they make use of fast films and high energy developers, are grainy to begin with. Overexposure only increases this.

In many instances, a slight textural quality of grain is desirable, as it produces a realistic quality. However, grain is not desirable if it is so large that it reduces the sharpness of the image.

In available light photography, shutter speeds are generally slow. It is, therefore, necessary to brace or support the camera during exposure. This minimizes the problem of movement. When there is a problem of movement, it is wise to make the exposure at the peak of action of the subject, as movement is less at that point. Camera movement, combined with subject movement, is one of the major causes of unsharpness in photographs made with available light.

Because maximum F/Numbers are used, depth of field is always shallow. Care in focusing is essential. When photographing people, it is advisable to focus on their eyes. If they are out of focus it is usually objectionable.

Printing negatives made with available light usually requires burning-in and dodging. Highlights and white areas tend to block up, and require burning-in to bring out the tones. The shadows, because of the small amount of exposure, tend to be thin and empty, and require dodging to retain the sparce detail.

CLOSE-UPS

A close-up photograph of an object is often quite exciting because it allows one to see images which are often ignored. We are constantly looking at objects, but how often do we pick one up for critical examination? Paul Strand and Edward Weston have produced very exciting photographs of ordinary objects such as cup and saucer, and vegetables, by photographing them close-up.

The term "close-up," as it will be discussed, is the distance from the camera to the subject, which is less than three and one half feet. The majority of the adjustable cameras allow photographs to be made at a close distance of three or four feet. "Suplementary lenses" may be attached to these cameras, enabling one to photograph objects considerably closer. These supplementary lenses are available in three different degrees of magnification. They may also be used in combinations in order to obtain extreme magnifications. The supplementary lens works on the same principle as the magnifing glass and is made with inexpensive optical glass which tends to reduce the image sharpness. Supplementary lenses do not require an exposure compensation, but should be used with the aperture closed down to F/8 or F/11. The following sketch illustrates how supplementary lenses may be attached to the camera lens.

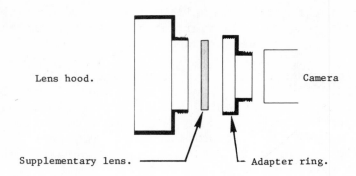

Lens hood.

Camera

Supplementary lens. ⎯⎯⎯⎯⎯

⎣⎯ Adapter ring.

FOCUSING FRAME AND CLOSE-UP STRING

Most view finders are relatively accurate to within three or four feet
from the subject. Closer than that, they are grossly inaccurate. The
use of a focusing frame, which is illustrated below, is useful in
remedying this.

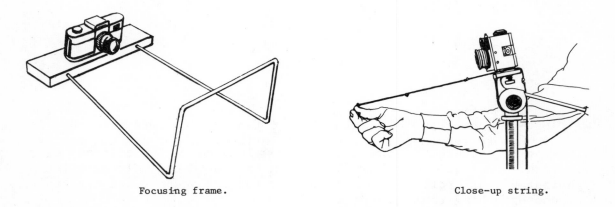

Focusing frame.

Close-up string.

The focusing frame may be tested with a piece of ground glass on the
film plane in order to check the area covered and focused, because
the distance from the camera to the subject is very critical with
close-ups. The closer the camera is to the subject, the more critical
the focus becomes. This focusing frame works well if only one distance
and degree of close-up is desired. However, it lacks versatility.

A piece of string may also be used to determine the areas in sharp
focus when photographing objects at close range. After the string
is fastened to the camera, knots are tied at the rear and fore limits
of focus. The string is stretched out, and as long as the subject
is between the two knots, it will be in sharp focus. This method is
not accurate because of parallax, but is cheap and easily assembled.

The twin lens reflex camera normally focuses up to only three and a half feet. However, there are accessory close-up lenses enabling photographs to be made as close as one foot. The first set enables photographs to be made from 19 to 34 inches, the second set from 13 to 19 inches, and the third set from 10 to 13 inches. Each set contains two lenses, one for the lens which allows for exposure and the other for the focusing lens. These lenses are corrected for parallax.

The majority of the more expensive 35 mm rangefinder cameras have accessories which convert these cameras into single lens reflexes. Such an accessory is called a "reflex housing". The reflex housing is attached to the camera in place of the lens and, in turn, is attached to a bellows unit into which the lens is fastened. See page 15.

The bellows allows a close-up ratio from 1:1 to 4:1. The ratio 1:1 means that the image size on the film is the same as the original (a one inch object is one inch on the negative). A 4:1 ratio means that the image size on the negative is four times larger than the original. The inserting of a different focal length lens also alters the degree of close-up coverage. A double cable release is necessary in order that the reflex mirror may be raised before exposing. The single lens reflex camera also accommodates a bellows unit, but is less cumbersome to operate as the reflex housing is not necessary.

Extension tubes are another means by which photographs may be made close-up. Extension tubes come in different lengths, and may be used singly or in combination, depending upon the degree of coverage desired. The extension tube is attached to the camera. The lens, in turn, is attached to the tube. See the following illustration.

Short extension tube.   Long extension tube.

The extension tube system is ideally suited for the single lens reflex camera, but may also be adapted to rangefinder cameras with a reflex housing in place of a bellows unit. An extension tube is less expensive than a bellows unit, but lacks versatility.

The best solution for close-up photography is the use of a single lens reflex camera or a view camera. With these cameras, one may actually see through the camera's lens, which eliminates all the problems of subject to camera distance, the degree of magnification and parallax.

When photographing objects close-up, the depth of field is very shallow. The single lens reflex camera and view camera allow one to actually see the depth of field. This is a visual experience which is more effective than consulting charts. Camera movement is a problem when photographing objects close-up. A tripod is always necessary.

The extension tubes and bellows units, by increasing the distance the light must travel in order to expose the film, require exposure increases. This is determined by an exposure factor, the number by which the normal exposure is multiplied, in order to obtain the correct exposure. For example, an exposure factor of 2X indicates that twice the normal exposure is required. A short extension tube has a smaller factor than a long one. The exposure factor is usually inscribed on the tube or included with the enclosed instructions. A bellows unit usually has an exposure factor scale which indicates the required exposure changes as the lens is moved in or out. It is important to remember these exposure factors. Otherwise, the film is underexposed.

The view camera, with its focusing through the lens and long bellows, is ideal for close-up photography. However, when the bellows is extended for close-ups, an exposure increase is necessary. View cameras do not have scales which indicate an increase in exposure, but the following may be used.

$$\frac{\text{Focal Length}^2 \text{ of the lens}}{\text{New Bellows}^2 \text{ extension}} = \frac{\text{Original exposure time}}{\text{New required exposure time}}$$

Example: Bellows Extension Exposure Increase Formula

A 4" x 5" view camera with a six inch lens is focused on an object. The bellows are extended twelve inches and the meter indicates an exposure of one second at F/32.

$$\frac{FL^2}{\text{New Bellows extension}^2} = \frac{\text{Original Exposure Time}}{X \text{ (new required exposure time)}}$$

$$\frac{6^2}{12^2} = \frac{1}{X} \qquad \frac{36}{144} = \frac{1}{X} \qquad 36X = 144 \qquad X = 4$$

The new exposure should be four at F/32.

The following technique accomplishes the same as the above formula without the use of a pencil and paper. It is done with the F/Number and shutter speed dials on an exposure meter. In the following example, assume the exposure to be 1 second at F/16. The camera has a 5 1/2 inch focal length lens and the bellows is extended 12 inches.

Indicated exposure: 1 second at F/16

Bellows extension: 12 inches

Focal length of lens: 5 1/2 inches

1. Obtain exposure in normal manner (1 second at F/16).

2. Measure the bellows extension (12 inches).

3. The F/Number scale is assumed to represent the focal length. Place the shutter speed (in this example, 1 second) opposite the 5.6. See the following illustration.

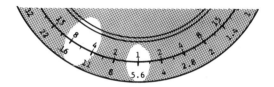

4. On the F/Number scale, find the F/Number which corresponds with the bellows extension. In this example a 12 inch bellows extension indicates 4 1/2 seconds. When encountering fractions (4 1/2 seconds) it is best to overexpose rather than underexpose. Thus 5 seconds at F/16 is the new corrected exposure.

Because the numbers do not always round out evenly, there are slight inaccuracies. These inaccuracies, however, are usually too minor to affect the exposure. The simplicity of the technique enables the bellows extension factor to be figured easily and quickly.

COMPENSATING DEVELOPERS

Compensating developers are usually highly concentrated liquids. They are "one-shot" developers. The concentrated stock solution is diluted before use, used, and discarded. There is no replenishment system. These developers help to minimize the contrast which is inherent in most thin emulsion films. The following is a list of thin emulsion films and compensating developers.

THIN EMULSION FILMS   COMPENSATING DEVELOPERS

Pan-X   (Kodak)   Plymouth Ethol T.E.C.
Verispan   (Ansco)   Edwal Minicol
K.B. 14   (German)   FR X-22
K.B. 21   (German)

These films may be used with any of the above developers to produce
the ultimate in quality. Because these films are slow, their application is restricted.

COPYING

Copying is often a form of close-up photography. The single lens reflex
camera and the view camera are ideal for this because there is no problem with parallax. The subject, whether it is a drawing, a photograph
or a painting, is assumed to be two-dimensional. A tripod, cable release
and two photofloods are all of the necessary equipment. The two photofloods are used to illuminate the material to be copied. They should
be evenly spaced and at a 45° angle. See the following illustration.

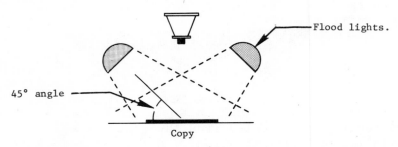

It is important that the lights are evenly spaced and that their distribution is uniform across the material. Check with an exposure
meter or use the following technique. Place a pencil on the material
at the center and compare the resulting shadows. If the shadows are
equal, the lighting is balanced.

The camera is placed in the center and is parallel to the copy. Sometimes when photographing a highly varnished subject the angle of the
lights may need to be changed. The angle is decreased in order to
help eliminate the glare. This is the exception, not the rule.

The exposure may be obtained with an incident or reflected light meter.
The incident meter, because it always reads only the incident light, is
ideal for copying. The sphere may be rotated to lessen the danger of
shadows from the meter or photographs. If the copy is darker or lighter
than the average, the difference in exposure must be estimated. The
reflected light meter should be read off an 18% neutral gray card. These
gray cards are readily available at photographic supply stores. Be careful not to have any shadows on the gray card when the reading is made.
The resulting exposure from this method will give an average range of
tones. Again, if the copy is extremely light or dark, compensation will
be necessary.

The black and white film used for copying is of two basic types, continuous tone film and high contrast film. The continuous tone film
is ordinary black and white panchromatic film, and may be used when-

ever a continuous tone copy is required. The high contrast film is
for copying drawings, type and other material which demands only a
strong black and white with no gray tones.

        Continuous tone film
          Panatomic - X
          Plus   - X

        High contrast film
          Kodalith

EXPOSING COLOR FILM

Although exposing color reversal transparencies does not involve complicated processes and preparation, it does necessitate a careful evaluation of one's light source. A small error in exposure of either too
much or too little exposure may drastically change color rendition. An
overexposed transparency produces colors which are pale, tints having a
washed out appearance, instead of shades. Underexposure produces a very
dark transparency having no detail, with dark, subdued colors.

The exposure latitude for color transparencies is considerably narrower
than that for black and white film. With color transparencies, an increase or decrease of 1/2 of an F/Number changes the appearance, whereas a change of two F/Numbers is possible with black and white film. As a
result, the accurate determination of exposure, with an exposure meter,
is essential. A variation in processing may be "over" or "under" to
the degree of changing the film speed by 1/2 an F/Number. For critical
color renditions, bracketing the exposure is recommended. Bracketing
involves making three different exposures of the same view of the subject. One exposure is made as determined by the exposure meter. The
second exposure is made by giving 1/2 an F/Number more exposure, the
third by giving 1/2 an F/Number less exposure. As a result, any slight
error in exposure determination, or variables in processing, may generally be eliminated. Of course, bracketing basically applies to studio
still lifes where there is little subject action.

The color of the light source is also an important consideration in
making color transparency exposures. Each light source has a different
dominant color. Daylight is dominantly blue, while artificial light
is red. The eye, because of its adaptability, is not aware of this
distinction. Color film is. As a result there are different color
films for the following types of illumination:

        Daylight   (Daylight)
        Professional Studio Equipment   (Type B)
        Photoflood   (Type A)

Because these films vary in color sensitivity, color filters are necessary if one type of film is to be used with a light source other than that for which it is corrected. There are conversion filters for combinations of film and light, as long as the combination is between artificial light sources, or between an artificial light source and daylight. The use of daylight film is not recommended for any artificial light situation because the necessary correction filter is so dark that the resulting exposures may not be practical. If, by accident, a film has been used with a light source other than that for which it had been intended, without correction filtration, the resulting transparency will be improperly exposed with inaccurate colors.

A light source's relative warmness (red, yellow) or coolness (green, blue) is designated by its degrees Kelvin. The cooler the color, the higher the degrees Kelvin (K). For example, type A film is 3400 K., whereas type B is 3200 K. Therefore, type A is corrected for a cooler source of light.

The following chart lists color correction filters for the various combinations of light and film:

Type of Film	Daylight Correction Filter	Type of Correction Filter	
		A	B
Type A	85		82A
Type B	85B	81A	

The A.S.A. numbers vary, depending on the filtration. The information furnished with the film may be consulted for specific solutions.

The use of an ultraviolet-haze filter (E.K. 1A) is recommended for photographing outdoor situations. This filter helps reduce atmospheric haze and helps to warm up the color in shadows. It does not require any exposure compensation.

DEVELOPING FILM BY INSPECTION

Panchromatic film must be developed in total darkness. In many instances this is a handicap. Sometimes a negative must be inspected during development, in order to see if it should be over or normally developed. Many photographers inspect their film as normal procedure. After 50% of the normal developing time, the negatives may be inspected with the prescribed safelight. The negative must be viewed by reflected light only. The negative must not be held up towards the safelight in an attempt to see through it. The film is opaque, and only the surface can be inspected.

This technique works for both roll and sheet film, but sheet film, by nature, is easier to handle. It may be necessary to cut roll film, with the danger of cutting a negative in half in the dark. Development by inspection is very difficult because it necessitates practice as well as an awareness of how the negatives should look when viewed under such dark conditions.

One method used in development by inspection involves a *desensitizer*. A desensitizer is a solution which desensitizes film, allowing the inspection of a negative with a fairly bright light. On examining a negative, one may decide if it has developed sufficiently, or requires additional time. The use of a desensitizer usually requires more initial film exposure, which reduces its practicality.

FILM PACK

A *film pack* is a package that contains sixteen sheets of film. The film pack is placed in a *film pack adapter* and is inserted in the back of a view or press camera in the same manner as a film holder. The film pack has paper tabs which are pulled as each exposure is made. This action moves the exposed film and replaces it with unexposed. The advantage of the film pack is that it is about the thickness of a single film holder but contains sixteen exposures. The difficulty with film pack is that the film is not as stiff as ordinary film, which makes it difficult to handle.

The developing of a film pack consists of opening it in total darkness and separating the film from the paper tabs. The film is taped to the tabs and care must be exercised to prevent tearing or creasing the film. Some photographers soak the film in water prior to development because of the films' flimsy nature. This reduces the danger of the film sticking together during development.

The handling of the dry film pack negatives is also more difficult than with ordinary sheet film. It has the tendency to "pop" during the exposure when enlarging. The negative becomes hot and expands, throwing the image out of focus. A glass negative carrier will prevent the negative from popping, but is more difficult to keep clean.

A film pack is more expensive than sheet film, but is useful whenever bulk or weight is a consideration.

FILTERS

Filters are colored pieces of glass placed in front of the lens to keep certain colors of light from reaching the film. They can thus be used in black and white photography to alter the rendition of a scene by changing the relative values of different colors. For example, a yellow filter allows yellow light and the neighboring colors on the spectrum to pass through but absorbs much of the blue light. Thus, when photographing a blue sky with a yellow filter, some of the light does not reach the film and the resulting print shows the sky as being darker than it would otherwise appear so that clouds are emphasized.

Filters may be used either to lighten or darken objects of a particular color. To lighten an object's tonal value a filter of the same color as the object is used. To darken it, as in the above case, a filter of the opposite color is used. Generally, yellow, red, orange and green filters are the most commonly used for black and white photography.

The following illustrations show how tone in the sky is effected by filters. The edge of the building is white and is not directly effected by the change in filters; thus the whites match in the various prints. In the first illustration (A), a blue filter was used to whiten the sky, and as a result there is no indication of clouds. The second illustration (B) was made with a yellow filter which slightly darkens the blue sky and shows the clouds. The third illustration (C) uses a red filter darkening the sky and making the clouds more pronounced. Besides changing the tone of the sky, notice how the rendition of the brick changes. As the sky becomes darker the bricks (reddish in color) become lighter. Before filters are used, the total situation must be analized because in order to gain one effect another is often lost.

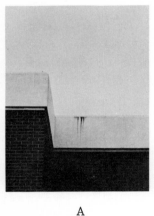 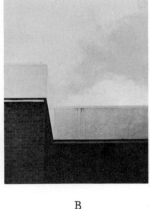 

A   B   C

In some situations, filters are needed to correct the film's inaccurate rendition of the values in a scene. This inaccuracy is due to the difference in color between tungsten and daylight illumination. Daylight is basically blue and tungsten is basically red. Panchromatic film is corrected for a situation in between and is generally used without filtration. However, for a very precise rendition under tungsten illumination, a green filter (X-1) must be used and a light yellow filter (K-2) is required outdoors.

The following illustration shows how a scene is effected by a dark red filter. The photographer wanted the scene to be slightly dark in order to emphasize the clouds. But the barn, because it was a dark red, is rendered as a black. There is no detail between sections of the barn. The use of a red filter produced the desired cloud effect but lightened the tone of the barn producing a more pleasing effect.

No filter.

Red filter.

CHARACTERISTICS OF COLOR FILTERS

Red A red filter will darken the sky drastically, and is usually used with Infrared film.

Blue A blue filter is used rarely because it lightens the sky.

Green A green filter darkens the sky, produces a more neutral rendition of foliage, and is often used with portraits.

Yellow A yellow filter darkens the sky and water. It is a commonly used filter.

Magenta and Cyan They are rarely used with black and white photography but are often used as color correction filters in color photography.

Orange An orange filter darkens the sky and water and helps to penetrate atmospheric haze.

102

The following includes a number of situations with filter suggestions:

Clouds against a blue sky

Natural	K-2 Yellow
Darker than natural	Wratten G Orange
Very dark	Wratten A Red

Consult "Infrared" for even more drastic renditions.

Water, blue sky

Natural	K-2 Yellow
Sky and water darker than natural	Wratten G Orange

Distant Landscape (Haze Penetration)

Natural	K-2 Yellow
Reduction of haze	Wratten G Orange
	Wratten A Red
Elimination of haze	Infrared film with Wratten A Red

Foliage

Natural	K-2 Yellow

Beaches, Snow

Natural textural	K-2 Yellow
Greater textural rendition	Wratten G Orange
	Wratten A Red

INFRARED

An infrared film, used in conjunction with a deep red filter, is sensitive to infrared radiation which is invisible to the unaided eye. The infrared film therefore "sees" things differently. It has the ability to penetrate atmospheric haze and to record details in the distance which are not visible to ordinary film and filters. The tonal rendition is, however, quite contrasty and greens such as foliage and grass, appear almost white, while blues become very dark.

Infrared

FILTER FACTOR

Filters, because they absorb light, require additional film exposure. This exposure compensation is called the *filter factor*, the number by which the normal exposure is multiplied to obtain the correct exposure. Note that the filter factor is different for daylight and tungsten illumination. This is due to the relative color balance of each light source. The following is a list of the generally used filters and the filter factors for black and white photography.

Filter Used		Color of Filter	Daylight Filter Factor	Tungsten Filter Factor
K-2	(8)	Yellow	2X	1.5X
X-1	(11)	Green	4X	3X
Wratten A	(25)	Red	8X	4X
Wratten G	(15)	Orange	3X	2X

A 2X filter factor indicates that twice the normal exposure is required for a particular filter. For example, the indicated exposure is 1/50 at F/8. The addition of a filter with a filter factor of 2X will require its exposure to be changed to 1/50 at F/5.6 or 1/25 at F/8. Either of these adjustments increase the exposure by 100%. The one (1/50 at F/5.6) changed the F/Number, whereas the other changed the shutter speed (1/25 at F/8). The choice of which needs changing depends on the subject to be photographed.

The manipulation of the F/Number is generally a most convenient manner of exposure adjustment. The following chart relates the filter factor to the increase of exposure by F/Number information.

Filter Factor	1.2	1.5	2	2.5	3	4	5	8
Increase in F/Number	1/3	2/3	1	1 1/3	1 2/3	2	2 1/3	3

Filters are available either in sheets of colored gelatin or encased in glass. They are attached to the front of the camera lens by adapter rings. The size of the filter is given a series number which indicates its diameter. A #4 filter is small in diameter, while a series #8 is much larger.

There are two other filters which, although they have not inherent color, are useful in both black and white and color photography. They are the *neutral density* filter and the *Polaroid* filter.

NEUTRAL DENSITY FILTER

A neutral density filter is a filter which appears gray and absorbs all color. It is used as a means of cutting down the amount of light entering the camera. In a few rare situations, a camera, in spite of its shutter speeds and F/Numbers, may not be able to control the brightness of the situation. One example might involve exposing a fast film at the beach. Even with a fast shutter speed and a very small aperture, the negative may still be overexposed. The use of the neutral density filter is the last resort in the attempt to reduce the amount of light entering the camera. These filters are available in different degrees of opacity.

POLA-FILTER

The pola-filter is a unique filter which filters glare but not color. Light, as it is reflected from subjects, is polarized (metalic subjects are the exception). This polarized light, reflecting from non-metallic surfaces, appears as a glare. The pola-filter is able, partially or completely, to remove this glare. The angle of the light source to the subject is an important factor in the pola-filter's ability to filter out this glare. At 30° the glare is completely removed, but at 90°, the filter has no effect.

The pola-filter may be used in the following manner. When viewing the subject, the pola-filter must be rotated slowly. One will notice that the glare gradually disappears. It is critical that one replaces the pola-filter in front of the lens with the same degree of rotation after the necessary adjustments are made. If the degree is not the same, the desired effect is lost. Some manufacturers provide a small pola-filter attached to the main pola-filter in order that the effect may be observed and adjusted without removing the pola-filter from the camera. The view camera or the single lens reflex camera allows one to easily see this adjustment, and they do not require a viewing pola-filter.

The ability of a pola-filter to remove glare from water and certain types of reflections is useful. The following two illustrations show a scene photographed with and without a pola-filter

Without pola-filter.   With pola-filter.

The pola-filter removes the glare from the marble, which gives the marble a more textured quality. The following two photographs illustrate how the reflections on a glass case are affected by a pola-filter.

Without pola-filter.

With pola-filter.

The reflections disappear, enabling one to see the contents of the case.

The pola-filter is especially useful in color photography. It allows for darkened sky, more dramatic clouds, and does not affect the overall color balance of the scene. Also, by reducing glare, the colors have a richer quality. The handicap of the pola-filter in color photography is its filter factor (2.5). Often, this factor, combined with a low light situation, prevents its use. However, color films are rapidly increasing in speed, allowing the pola-filter to be used more often.

FINE GRAIN

The term "fine grain" refers to a film-developer combination which produces the least amount of grain. With small negatives, grain often presents a problem in making extreme enlargements. Grain, when it is extremely large, reduces the sharpness of a photograph. As a result, the quality of the photograph suffers.

The following is a list of fine grain films and developers:

Fine Grain Films

   Panatomic - X

   Plus - X Pan

   K.B. 21

Fine Grain Developers

   Microdol - X

   Edwal Super 12 or 20

   Magee and Baker (British) Promicrol

Any of the above films may be used with the above developers to produce fine grain without any sacrifice in speed of the film. However, the ultimate in quality is obtained with *thin emulsion films* and *compensating developers*.

INTENSIFICATION AND REDUCTION

Often, due to an error in exposure or development, negatives are made which are very thin or extremely opaque. The technical quality is too poor to yield satifactory prints. These negatives may sometimes be salvaged through the use of an *intensifier* or a *reducer*. A thin, under-developed negative requires intensification. A thick, opaque negative may be reduced with a reducer. These two techniques should be thought of as "last ditch" attempts to save a negative. The technique is often tricky, and is not a substitute for proper technique.

Intensification increases the opacity of a negative. Basically, it compensates for underdevelopment, with slight correction for under-exposure. There are three types of intensifiers.

1. Subproportional Intensifier. Opacity in the shadow areas is im-proved.

2. Proportional Intensifiers. Most often used, this intensifier helps correct underexposure and underdevelopment.

3. Superproportional Intensifier. This intensifier increases opacity in the highlights, increasing contrast.

The permanence of many intensifiers is not dependable. The image eventu-ally fades.

Reduction has the ability to reduce the opacity of a negative. Both Ansco and Kodak have easily mixed preparations. There are three types of reducers.

1. Contrast Reducer. This reducer affects the shadow areas of the negative, bringing about more contrast. It is basically used for over-exposed negatives.

2. Proportional Reducer. Contrast remains the same, while the overall opacity of a negative is reduced. It is used when a negative is too opaque for enlarging.

3. Superproportional Reducer. This reducer affects highlights, decreases contrast, and is very tricky to control.

A negative to be reduced must be thoroughly fixed and washed. The obser-vation of reduction is difficult, as a wet negative appears slightly dif-ferent from a dry one. It is necessary to treat one negative at a time. Immediately after reduction the negative must be washed. Complete in-structions accompany the packaged reducers.

Intensifiers and reducers should only be used if there is no opportunity for making another negative.

MONO-BATH DEVELOPERS

A mono-bath developer is a combination developer-fixer which develops and fixes the film in one operation. Mono-bath developers are purchased in liquid form and are "one-shot" developers. Using a mono-bath developer, the film speed is somewhat reduced. The quality is also not as good as that provided by conventional developers. However, for extreme speed in processing, the mono-bath developers are useful. The following lists the two available mono-bath developers:

> Cormar Unibath   cc-1
>   recommended for slow film
>
> Cormar Unibath   cc-2
>   recommended for fast film

POLAROID

The introduction, in 1947, of the Polaroid-Land process initiated a new concept in photography. No longer must the photographer wait until his return to the dark room to see the results of his efforts. This lapse in time between exposure, processing and printing has troubled photographers, both technically and esthetically. The Polaroid-Land process enables the photographer to see the results where he is photographing

Polaroid film is exposed in a normal manner. After exposure, the film is pulled through rollers which squeeze out a jelly-like substance which develops and fixes the image. The processing is done in the camera, and only requires a time of about ten seconds. Upon completion, the back of the camera is opened, the negative is peeled away from the positive, and a full tone black and white print is obtained. Originally the negatives could not be saved. Now, with a specific type of Polaroid film, only available for the 4 x 5 sheet film size, the negative may be saved and printed in a normal manner. To insure permanence, the print is coated with a substance which also protects its surface.

The major difficulty with the Polaroid-Land process is the problem of duplicate or additional prints of a given exposure. The original must be rephotographed, which is expensive, and image quality is lost.

In 1963, color Polaroid-Land film was introduced. The variety of Polaroid-Land film materials which are available lend themselves not only to the amateur or professional market, but also to the specific needs of scientific documentation (infrared, oscilliscope recording).

SHEET FILM

The view camera is designed to accommodate sheet film. Sheet film is, as the name implies, film in sheet form. The common sizes are 4" x 5",

5" x 7", and 8" x 10". A few smaller sizes are still available, such as 2 1/4" x 3 1/4" and 3 1/4" x 4 1/4". Sheet film is stiffer than roll film, and is loaded into film holders. The film holder is a device which accommodates two sheets of film, one on each side, separated by an opaque barrier.

An opaque *slide* prevents the film from being exposed accidentally. The holder is placed in the back of the camera, and the slide nearest the lens is pulled out. It is important that the shutter of the camera is closed. The film is exposed as the shutter is clicked. The slide is then inserted back into the holder, and the holder removed. The slides have a white and black side. The white side indicates unexposed film, and the black side indicates an empty or exposed side.

LOADING OF FILM HOLDERS

Both sides are first removed from the holders and placed on a clean table. Holders should be brushed and all dirt, lint and dust removed. A wide, soft paintbrush is helpful in cleaning holders. Compressed air, if available, is also effective. It is important not to deposit moisture when blowing off the dust orally. The holders and film should be organized before the lights are turned out. Each piece of film has a notch in the upper right hand corner which prevents it from being loaded into the holder the wrong way. See the following illustration.

Plus-X Pan   Infrared

Notice that the notches are different. Each type of film has its own unique notch, making identification possible in total darkness. It is important to load the holders with the emulsion side up, with the notch in the upper right hand corner. Failure to load holders correctly results in blank (unexposed) film. The film is held in the right hand and by its edges. One may check the notch with the index finger to insure its proper position. See the following illustration.

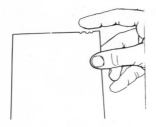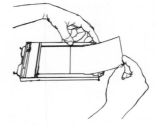

The film is carefully inserted under the two retainers of the holder which is held by the left hand. It is gently pushed into place. Its placement may be checked by lifting the film gently to make sure that it is secured by the retainers. The holder hinge is then pressed down and the slide inserted. See the illustration on the previous page.

When the holder is loaded with two sheets of unexposed film, both white sides of the slides should be showing. After both exposures, the black sides of the slides should be showing. In this manner, a holder, on examination, will indicate if it is exposed, partially exposed, or empty. Careful attention to this will result in less confusion, as well as less chance of accidentally making a double exposure or exposing a holder which is empty.

The purpose and advantage of sheet film is that each sheet may be developed separately. The exposure, development and manipulation may be best accomplished with sheet film. Sheet film, because of its individual development, allows for the ultimate in quality.

SHEET FILM - DEVELOPING PROCEDURE

The developing of sheet film is similar to the developing of a print. A series of four trays are arranged in a row, followed by a means of washing the film. Film (panchromatic), because it is sensitive to all light, is processed in TOTAL DARKNESS.

Water.   Developer.   Stop bath   Hypo

On the extreme left, the first tray contains water and is used to wet the film prior to development. If only one or two sheets of film are to be developed, this step may not be necessary. The use of this tray is also debatable, as some photographers make use of it while others do not.

The second tray contains the developer. The type and brand is dependent on the film. Developers such as D-76 and U.F.G. are satisfactory for most films. The third tray contains water or a diluted acid solution (stop bath). If plain water is used, it should be changed after each batch of film has been processed. In counteracting the action of the developer, water alone is not as effective as a stop bath.

The fourth tray contains the hypo (fix). The hypo used for film is more concentrated than that used for paper, usually twice the concentration.

The temperature of all solutions should be in the range of 68° to 75°F. The development time depends on the particular film and developer being used. The information packaged with the film developer may be consulted for specific developing time. The chemicals must be prepared and organized before turning out the room lights.

The exposed negatives are removed from the holders IN TOTAL DARKNESS, and placed in the first tray. There they are agitated in order to prevent one from sticking to another. The manner of agitation throughout the development process includes sliding the bottom negative out from under the pile, laying it down gently on the others, and carefully pushing the entire pile down into the solution. This should be repeated a few times to insure that one piece of film is not sticking to the other. Using only one hand, a negative is then lifted from the tray, drained momentarily and transferred to the other hand. Using the other hand, the film is inserted into the developer. The timer, which was preset before the lights were turned out, is then turned on. Again, the length of time is dependent upon the type of film, the developer and the temperature of the developer. It is extremely important that the film be agitated when it enters the developer. If it is not, bubbles may form which cause areas of the film to be unevenly developed. The manner of agitation has been outlined previously. A rhythm of agitation should be established which is not too fast or too slow, and which continues for the entire time of development. Upon completing the development, the negatives are (one by one) transferred to the stop bath where they remain for about three seconds. In the same manner, the negatives are then placed in the hypo (fix) and agitated. After about a minute, the room lights may be turned on. The film remains in the hypo for about five minutes.

The washing of sheet film is best accomplished in film hangers. Film hangers are made out of stainless steel, each holding one sheet of film. These hangers allow for the washing and handling of sheet film with less chance of scratches. A number of hangers may be grouped together for washing. Film hangers may also be used to develop sheet film, but with the tray method one is less prone to have developing streaks and mottling. In washing there must be rapid change of water. The washing tank must be periodically dumped to insure satisfactory washing. See the following illustration.

Film hanger

After the film has been washed for twenty minutes, the negatives may be removed from the hangers and placed in a wetting agent (photo-flo). Excess solution is wiped off the negatives with a sponge or surgical cotton, moistened with the wetting agent. The negatives are then hung up to dry as the above diagram illustrates. The separate pieces of film must be spaced so that they do not come in contact with each other while they are drying.

STROBE - ELECTRONIC FLASH, FLASH BULBS

The first photographers were only able to photograph on bright sunny days because the speed of the materials was very slow. Gradually, the sensitivity of the films was improved and other means of illumination were developed. One of the first means, and perhaps the most dramatic, was the use of *flashpowder*. Flashpowder is a compound of chemicals which literally ignite, producing a bright flash of light accompanied by a large cloud of smoke. Flashpowder was highly unpredictable and quite dangerous.

FLASH BULBS

The development of incandescent light replaced the sky lighting techniques in the studio, but was little help for the photographer who needed a portable light source. Flashpowder was used until the introduction of the *flash bulb*. A flash bulb is a glass bulb filled with a magnesium ribbon which produces a flash of intense light when subjected to electricity. A flash bulb provides only one flash but is safe, dependable and easier to carry than flashpowder.

The light produced by flash bulbs has a tendency to be very directional. In the beginning, subjects were over-exposed and isolated from their surroundings. Too often the photographer was content with the flash bulb mounted directly on the camera. Gradually, photographers began to use flash bulbs at different positions off the camera in order to control the resulting shadows. The flash bulb, when held slightly higher and away from the camera, casts the shadows out of the picture area.

As the sensitivity of films increased and as flash bulbs became brighter, the use of *bounce light* became practical. With this technique, the flash is directed off the ceiling or walls. The ceiling acts as a giant reflector, distributing light over a broad area, giving a more natural appearance to the photograph. It is also less uncomfortable for the subject, as spots in front of the eyes, which result from direct flash, are eliminated.

Later, in the 1930's, *strobe - electronic* flash was introduced. Strobe is an electronic device consisting of a battery, capacitors and flash tube which stores up energy that may be released periodically. The release of this energy produces a very bright flash for a fraction of a second (1/1000 of a second). In fact, the camera's ability to stop motion is determined by this short flash of light. The strobe provides a means with which photographs may be made of activities not normally visible such as a bullet in flight or the fluttering of a hummingbird.

Negatives exposed with a strobe require about 30% additional time in development. A strobe bulb is good for hundreds of flashes, is more practical for complicated lighting situations, and is, in the long run, cheaper.

The same principle of bounce light may be used to even greater advantage with the strobe. Strobes are more powerful than flash bulbs, and their ability to stop action is a valuable contribution. Originally, strobes were very heavy and expensive, but this is no longer the case.

Both the flash bulb and the strobe have guide numbers, enabling one to determine the correct exposure. As the subject and light distance increases, less light reaches the subject. The respective guide number (each type of film has a different guide number because of their difference in the A.S.A. numbers) is divided by the distance between the subject and the light source. For example, the guide number is 160 and the subject is ten feet from the light source (either flash bulbs or strobe). The correct exposure for this example is F/16.

THIN EMULSION FILMS

A thin emulsion film's emulsion is thinner than that of a regular film, and possesses finer particles of silver. As a result, there is less light dispersed through the thin emulsion during enlarging and the finer grain produces better quality. However, these films tend to be contrasty and rather slow. See section entitled "Compensating Developers" for additional information.

THREE DIMENSION - STEREO

In the search for realism the idea existed that if two pictures were seen, one for each eye, there would be an illusion of *three-dimensions*. Attempts to draw or paint these pictures failed, due to inaccuracies with the drawings. Photography eliminated this problem, and from the very start there was an interest in stereo. Stereo consists of two photographs, usually made with a camera which consists of two cameras combined. This combined camera closely approximates the vision of the human eye. The photographs when viewed through a viewer have a strong three-dimensional illusion. The interest in stereo has gone up and down over the years, but was especially popular in the early 1900's. It was the "home movies" of that period.

TONING

Toning is a technique which the early photographers, and even some
present day pictorialists, have used. Pictorialists have toned sea-
scapes blue and sunsets sepia. Commercial portrait photographers
also have often toned their portraits.

Toning is an attempt to produce color in photography, using black and
white materials in altering the relative color of photographs. A toned
photograph, in place of a gray, black and white photograph, may offer
dark brown or sepia tones. A photograph may be toned blue, green or
tan. However, too often the technique has been used in an attempt to
give meaning to an otherwise uninteresting photograph.

Frederick Sommer, Ansel Adams and other photographers use a modified
toning technique to slightly change the image color of their prints.
In place of warm (brown-blacks), the blacks are toned to produce cooler
blacks (blue-blacks). With this technique, blacks become richer (darker),
without any effect on the other tones. Toning reacts best with warm-
toned papers. Cold toned papers are hardly affected. This type of
toning is a modest form of toning. It must not be confused with the
techniques used by early or pictorial photographers. The image tone
of the photograph is only slightly changed because the toner is diluted. The process is described below.

The prints which are to be toned are first made slightly darker than
normal. A thorough wash is necessary before any toning may be attempted.
Stains result if the prints contain any hypo. Upon completion of the
washing the prints are bleached slightly in a dilute solution of potas-
ium ferricyonide. This solution is pale yellow in color. The prints
are then washed for thirty minutes and toned in a dilute solution of
selenium toner (one part toner to sixteen parts water). Prints are agitated in the toner, and then removed in approximately two minutes, when
they appear to be a shade darker than that which is desired. The prints
lighten slightly after they have been washed for an hour. A simplified
variation of this technique involves merely toning the washed prints in
a dilute solution of selenium toner (one part toner to sixteen parts water).
After the prints have been treated with this solution, they must again
be washed for an hour. Although the above techniques are somewhat elaborate, the difference between a toned print and one which is not, is
appreciated in comparison.

TWO-BATH DEVELOPER

A Two-Bath developer is a recent product named Diafine. Diafine is a
rather unique film developer in that it has the same developing time
for all films, regardless of film speed. Diafine may be used within
a temperature range of 70° - 85°F. A minimum developing time of two
minutes, and a maximum time of eight minutes may be used. Furthermore,
there is no prescribed time for any temperature. And the solution never needs replenishing.

The film is immersed in the first solution (A) for at least two minutes (maximum five minutes), and gently agitated. Upon completion, drain; do not rinse. Immerse in the second solution (B) for at least two minutes (maximum five minutes), and gently agitate. The film is then drained and immediately placed in hypo, without the usual fifteen second stop bath. The film is washed and dried in the normal manner.

UNDER-OVER FILM DEVELOPING

The photographer has two important variables which he may manipulate, the exposure and the development of the negative. The product of each variable, and how it affects the other, enables the photographer to increase or decrease the effective contrast of the subject.

The photographic printing paper is available in four or five different contrasts. Contrast #1 is very flat, that is, there is a wide range of gray tones between black and white. Contrast #4 has very few tones of gray between black and white. As a result, it is to the photographer's advantage to have his negatives print on #2 paper, in order to take advantage of the more abundant tonal range. However, all situations are not of average contrast. Some situations are rather flat due to the value rendition or illumination, while others are very contrasty. The photographer, using the following technique, may adjust the sensitivity of the film to make use of this wide range in value.

A photographer, when photographing subjects of average tonal range, will find that normal exposure and normal development produce a satisfactory negative. Slight changes in contrast may be obtained in printing with the different contrast papers. A problem arises in an attempt to photograph an extremely contrasty subject. Normal exposure and normal development may produce a negative which is too contrasty for compensation through the use of a less contrasty printing paper. The overall contrast range in the negative must be lowered. By purposely overexposing and slightly underdeveloping, the resulting negative will have less contrast and will produce a more satisfactory print. Usually twice the normal exposure and 1/3 less development is satisfactory. Negative inspection while developing is especially useful in this situation. The other extreme, involving a situation of little contrast, may require slight underexposure of one F/Number (1/2 the normal exposure) and 30% overdevelopment is suggested. Again, inspection while developing is useful. This technique is especially useful to the photographer using sheet film, because each sheet may be handled separately. The person using roll film usually must treat all the exposures on the roll in an equal manner, which normally is not practiced.

VARIABLE CONTRAST PAPER

Variable contrast paper is an enlarging (projection) paper which contains two emulsions. These two emulsions are sensitive to different colors. The different colors alter the variable contrast paper's range of tones. A yellow filter produces a wide range of tones (flat), whereas a blue filter limits the range of tones (contrast). There are also filters between these two extremes, allowing for a wide range of contrasts.

Light passing through a negative, and projected upon the variable contrast paper, is filtered. The manner of filtration depends upon the design of the enlarger. Some enlargers have provision for the filters above the condensers. This system is ideal because the handling and condition of the filters is not critical as it is in the other method. Enlargers which do not have provision for filters above the condensers must be adapted in order to hold the filters below the lens. Some enlargers, for example, the Omega enlargers, have a bracket below the lens on which the filter may be placed. This is the general method of filtration which often produces problems. The filter is often in the way of adjusting the aperture. It tends to obstruct the light coming out of the lens. Filters must also be kept spotlessly clean, because any dust, dirt, lint, etc. on the filter soften the projected image.

There are two types of variable contrast paper available on the domestic market. Varigam, a duPont product, and Polycontrast, produced by Eastman Kodak, are available. Basically, they are the same, with only slight differences in color tonality. Varigam is a cooler toned paper than Polycontrast.

Variable contrast paper, because it is sensitive to a wider range of tones than graded papers, usually requires special safelights. The majority of safelights for graded papers fog variable contrast paper, while the safelights for variable contrast paper do not fog the graded papers. Therefore, if variable contrast paper is used, or a variety of papers are used (such as in a school situation), the use of variable contrast paper safelights is recommended.

The color of the filters for variable contrast paper ranges from yellow to blue. As a result, the opacity varies from filter to filter. In practice, this means that the exposures must be altered as the filters are changed. For example, if the correct exposure with a yellow filter is 15 seconds, a 30-45 second exposure may be required using a blue filter. Eastman Kodak provides an exposure computer, a scale which indicates the new exposure when there is a change in the filters used. DuPont's new Varigam system has eliminated the change in opacity between their filters, with the exception of the darkest blue. This filter requires twice the normal exposure.

The advantage of variable contrast paper is that the photographer's variety of materials may be reduced. That is, one package of variable contrast paper, instead of one graded package of each of the four or five different contrasts required, is sufficient. The use of variable contrast paper instead of graded paper also allows one to print certain negatives more successfully. For example, it may be a very contrasty subject. The attempt to print for middle and dark tones, and then burn-in the white tones, is not always successful. The burning-in may be too drastic, resulting in uneveness of tones. The use of variable contrast paper may be more effective in handling this type of situation. A filter for the normal areas may be used for the initial exposure. A filter of lower contrast may then be very carefully substituted for the burning-in of the white areas. In this manner, the extreme range of tones may be handled most effectively, by changing contrast instead of merely exposure.

VIEW CAMERA MOVEMENTS

A view camera which uses a rising and sliding front and back and which has swings and tilts, enables the photographer to manipulate perspective and control depth of field. These adjustments, combined with the use of a large negative and individualized processing, provide the photographer with great control over the final image of the photograph.

A view camera may be swiveled on the lens axis both vertically and horizontally.

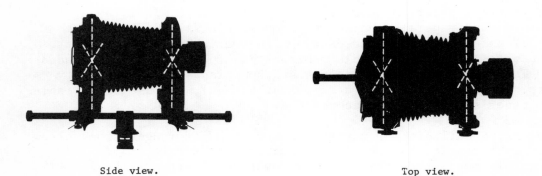

Side view.   Top view.

The back (A) is swung horizontally or tilted vertically to control the perspective of the image on the ground glass. As long as the ground glass (camera's back) is parallel to the subject, the image on the ground glass will be parallel to the subject. The front (B) allows the camera lens to be placed in the proper relationship with the subject for sharp focus. The basic principle for all view cameras is that the back of the camera is designed for perspective control, while the front of the camera is designed for controlling depth of field.

RISING AND SLIDING FRONT

The rising and sliding front enables the photographer to alter his viewpoint without moving the camera. These movements are very useful whenever an obstruction prevents the camera from being placed in the desired location. See the following illustration.

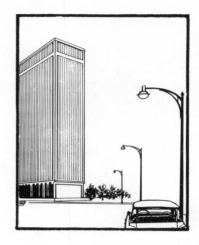

The rising and sliding front is only able to accommodate small degrees
of correction. In other situations where a greater degree of correction is needed, the use of tilts and swings is required.

TILTS AND SWINGS

Tilts and swings are used to correct the perspective and depth of
field of a subject. When the front and back of the camera are parallel to the subject, only a small portion of the building is visible
(sketch A). When the camera is pointed up, the entire building is
included but it has the appearance of falling back (sketch B). The
vertical lines of the building are not parallel and tend to converge
to a point.

A

B

By tilting the rear until it is parallel to the building, the vertical lines of the building become parallel (sketch B). But there is a problem with focusing. Portions of the building are so out of focus that even closing the aperture all the way down will not bring them into focus (sketch C).

When the front is made parallel to the building, the problem of focus disappears (sketch D). The rendition is now natural and clearly defined.

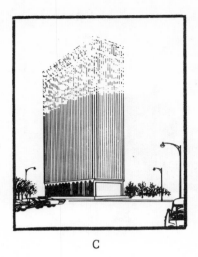

C

D

The front of the camera is often tilted in order to gain maximum depth of field on a horizontal plane, for example when it is desirable to have sharp focus from very near the camera to infinity. By tilting the front down slightly, the increase in depth of field will enable this to be accomplished. This technique works well with subjects such as fields but not with scenes containing vertical objects. These vertical objects will be greatly out of focus.

The use of swings offers the same control as the tilts, but does it by swinging horizontally instead of vertically. It therefore controls depth of field and perspective on a vertical plane. Often the situation requires that both tilts and swings be used.

WEIGHT AND TEMPERATURE-

CONVERSION CHART

The following charts correlate the two common systems of liquid and solid measurement. They make it possible to convert formulas from one system into the other.

U.S. LIQUID TO THE METRIC

Gallons	Quarts	Ounces	Drams, fluid	Liters
1	4	128	1024	3.79
.25	1	32	256	.95
		1	8	.03
.26	1.06	33.81	270.5	1

AVOIRDUPOIS TO METRIC

Pounds	Ounces	Grains	Grams	Kilograms
1	16	700	458.6	.45
.06	1	437.5	28.35	.028
		1	.0648	
	.04	15.43	1	.001
2.21	35.27	1540	1000	1

APPENDIX II

Insufficient agitation; formation of spots.

Tank not full; partial development.

NEGATIVE DEFECTS

ABRASIONS, MARKS OR STREAKS

Appearance: Fine, black lines, usually resembling pencil lines, are present on the film, may run the length of the film.

Cause: The lines are caused by friction on the emulsion of the film while the film is moved through the camera. This often occurs with an inexpensive camera. A 35 mm cassette which happens to have a small piece of dirt between the pieces of felt may scratch the film as it is removed or re-turned.

Remedy: The rough area must be located and made smooth. The inside of the camera should be cleaned periodically. The con-dition of the felt of 35 mm cassette should also be checked, especially if there is reloading of bulk film.

AIR BUBBLES

Appearance: When an air bubble occurs during film develop-ment, the area shows as a small, transparent spot.

Cause: The spot is caused by a bubble of air on the surface of the emulsion, which prevents the developer from coming in contact with the emulsion.

Remedy: See page 63 . To prevent air bubbles, the film must be agitated vigorously during the first few moments in order to dislodge any bubbles. Agitation must then continue per-iodically during the remaining developing time for five second intervals every 30 seconds.

BLOCKING

Appearance: A dark, heavy area of a negative which lacks any detail is blocked.

Cause: Extreme overexposure produces areas on a negative so dense that light cannot penetrate them. These areas are opaque, lack texture, and usually halation.

Remedy: Accurate determination of exposure and correct developing time.

BLURRED NEGATIVES

Appearance: Lack of sharpness of the negative image.

Cause: 1. The negative may not have been properly focused. 2. There may have been subject movement. 3. Camera movement. 4. Moisture, haze or a dirty lens may have been a factor.

Remedy: 1. The camera must be carefully held and focused. 2. The lens must be dirt-free.

BROWN SPOTS

Appearance: Brown spots on the negative.

Cause: Prior to development, oxidized developer or fine particles of chemicals may settle on the film. This may also occur from rust in the work water.

Remedy: 1. The use of exhuasted developer must be avoided. 2. Fine particles of developer may be suspended in the air and settle on the film. This is a larger problem for sheet film than for roll film. 3. Filtering the work water removes all rust and impurities.

CRYSTALINE SURFACE

Appearance: The surface of the negative emulsion has a crystaline appearance, suggesting frost on a window pane.

Cause: The wash time has been insufficient causing the hypo to remain in the film and crystalize.

Remedy: The washing time must be sufficient.

EXCESSIVE CONTRAST

Appearance: Highlights, and even the middle gray tones, are rendered greatly out of proportion to the original subject.

Cause: The negatives have been overdeveloped.

Remedy: Negatives must be properly developed.

FADING TENDENCY

Appearance: Sepia or yellow colored stains are present.

Cause: Fixation or washing time has been insufficient.

Remedy: Fixing and washing of film must be done properly. The final wash is as important as any other operation in film development.

FINGER MARKS

Appearance: Imprint of fingers occurs on the negative.

Cause: The film has been touched with wet or greasy fingers before or during development.

Remedy: Hands must be kept clean and dry. Handle negatives by the edges only.

FLATNESS

Appearance: There is insufficient contrast between the highlights, middle gray tones, and shadows in the negative reproduction of the subject.

Cause: Flatness is usually caused by underdevelopment. However, the contrast of the subject or the lighting may originally have been of a flat nature.

Remedy: Film must be developed for the proper amount of time.

FOG

Appearance: Fog is a deposit of silver which does not allow part of the image to form. It may be very dense or slightly veiling. Fog increases the density and lowers the contrast of a negative. There are three types: aerial, dichoric, and light.

Cause: The negative may have been exposed to air during development. If the fog has a pinkish cast, there may have been a slight remainder of hypo in the film. The film, if panchromatic, may have been developed in total darkness.

Remedy: Keep the film totally submerged during development, keep solutions free of contamination, and develop panchromatic film in total darkness.

HALATION

Appearance: A dark area is present on the negative, extending from the area of intensely bright objects, suggesting a double image, and appearing as a halo or star on the print.

Cause: An intensely bright subject has been photographed by dark objects.

Remedy: Pointing the camera directly at a very bright source of light (the sun, street lights at night) must be avoided.

LINES SUGGESTING LIGHTNING

Appearance: Forked or branched lines appear on the negative, resembling lightning.

Cause: Static electricity has been produced in fast winding or rewinding of the film.

Remedy: The film must be wound and rewound slowly.

NEGATIVE TOO DENSE

Appearance: The negative appears rather opaque.

Cause: Overexposure, overdevelopment, or a combination of the two has occurred.

Remedy: Exposure and development must be correct.

NEGATIVE TOO THIN

Appearance: The negative has a pale, washed-out appearance.

Cause: Underexposure or underdevelopment, or a combination of the two has occurred.

Remedy: Exposure and development must be correct.

PINHOLES

Appearance: Minute, transparent spots occur on the negative.

Cause: Dust has been present on the film before exposure.

Remedy: The camera must be dust free. The film must be handled properly.

PURPLE DISCOLORATION

Appearance: Purple-colored stains are present on the film.

Cause: Stain occurs when negatives are allowed to stick together in the fixing bath (sheet film).

Remedy: Negatives must be properly agitated in the fixing bath.

RETICULATION

Appearance: The gelatin emulsion is either wrinkled or has a leather-like graininess.

Cause: There has been too great a difference in the temperature of the chemicals or the final wash.

Remedy: All solutions must be used within the prescribed temperature tolerance.

REVERSAL OF THE IMAGE

> Appearance: A positive image occurs when the negative is viewed by transmitted light.
>
> Cause: Extreme underexposure is the cause. The negative is too thin to print.
>
> Remedy: The exposure of the film must be correct.

SPOTS

> Appearance: Spots may be transparent, opaque, or semiopaque depending upon the cause of each. They may be vaguely or sharply defined.
>
> Cause: Transparent spots indicate an absence of silver deposit and are usually caused by dust on the film during exposure. The dust prevents the light from exposing the film. Floating chemical dust may settle on the film prior to development, and destroy the film's sensitivity. Opaque or semiopaque spots result from actual pieces of dirt being imbedded into the emulsion.
>
> Remedy: The camera must be kept clean. Mixing chemicals in the same room used for processing should be avoided. If possible, the wash water should be filtered.

STREAKS

> Appearance: Streaks or patches may be dark, white, or transparent.
>
> Cause: Dark streaks or patches are usually due to improper agitation in the developer. Contamination of chemicals results in light patches. A tear drop streak is caused by water splashing upon the film which has been hung up to dry.
>
> Remedy: Precautions which must be taken to avoid streaks suggest themselves when the cause is found.

UNEVEN DEVELOPMENT

> Appearance: Variations in densities of certain areas of the negative occur.
>
> Cause: Inconsistent or too active agitation while developing the film.
>
> Remedy: Agitate slowly and consistently.

YELLOW STAINS

Appearance: Areas of the negative have been stained yellow.

Cause: 1. The hypo may have been weak. 2. The developer may have been contaminated with hypo. 3. The negative may not have been sufficiently covered with hypo in fixing.

Remedy: Check the above causes and correct.

PRINT DEFECTS

Overexposure-underdeveloped print.

Print left in hypo too long.

ABRASIONS, MARKS OR STREAKS

Appearance: Tiny black lines, scratches.

Cause: Scratching the emulsion with print tongs while developing the print, or when cutting the paper with a paper cutter.

Remedy: Touch only the white border areas with the print tongs. Handle the paper carefully when using the paper cutter.

BAD DEFINITION, BLURRED

Appearance: The print is not sharply defined.

Cause: 1. In contact printing, the negative and paper may not be in perfect contact. 2. In enlarging, the negative may not be focused properly. 3. The enlarger may have vibrated during the exposure. 4. The negative may have been magnified excessively.

Remedy: 1. Make sure the negative and paper are in perfect contact in contact printing. 2. In enlarging, make sure the negative is focused properly. 3. Eliminate vibrations of the enlarger during the exposure. 4. Do not enlarge the negative excessively.

BLISTERS

Appearance: Tiny blisters on the surface of the print.

Cause: Softening of the emulsion causes blisters. The wash water was too hot.

Remedy: Do not wash prints for more than an hour. Keep the wash water temperature within the range of 68° - 75°F.

BROWN SPOTS AND STAINS

Appearance: Brown spots, stains on the print.

Cause: Rust in the wash water may cause stains. Exhausted developer, lacking an acid stop bath, and a weak fixing bath are other causes.

Remedy: Filter the wash water. Use only fresh developer, acid stop bath and fixing baths.

EXCESSIVELY DARK PRINTS

Appearance: The tones of the print are too dark.

Cause: Overexposure or overdevelopment of the print may produce excessive darkness.

Remedy: Reduce the exposure and do not overdevelop.

EXCESSIVELY LIGHT PRINTS

Appearance: The tones of the print are too light.

Cause: Underexposure or underdevelopment of the print may cause excessive lightness.

Remedy: Increase the exposure

FADING TENDENCY

Appearance: The image on the print is becoming too dark (fading).

Cause: Fading may result from an incomplete fixation, a prolonged fixation in weak hypo, and insufficient washing.

Remedy: Use only fresh chemicals and observe the proper immersion times.

FINGERPRINTS

Appearance: A white or black fingerprint on the finished print.

Cause: Wet, moist or chemically contaminated fingers in contact with the print surface may mar the print.

Remedy: Keep hands clean and dry.

FLATNESS

Appearance: The tones in the print are basically gray, lacking a pure white or a rich black.

Cause: The use of wrong contrast paper for a particular negative results in an often undesirable quality of flatness.

Remedy: Use the proper contrast paper for the particular negative.

FOG

Appearance: A slight fog grays down the tones of a print. A heavy fog darkens the overall tonality of the print.

Cause: 1. The safelight may be too close to the paper. 2. The paper may be exposed. 3. The paper may be out of date. 4. The print may have been developed too long. 5. The developer may have been contaminated.

Remedy: Check the above causes and correct.

MUDDY TONES

Appearance: The print has a poor tonal range. The black areas are gray and have a mottled appearance.

Cause: Overexposure, insufficient development, and outdated paper may cause muddy tones.

Remedy: Adjust the exposure in order that the print may be developed for 1 1/2 to 2 minutes. Do not use old, outdated paper.

SPOTS, BLACK

Appearance: The print has black spots.

Cause: A print made from a negative which has pinholes has black spots.

Remedy: See spotting.

SPOTS, WHITE

Appearance: The print has white spots.

Cause: 1. Hypo may have been accidentally splashed on the print prior to exposure and development. 2. Dust, dirt, etc. on the negative.

Remedy: 1. Do not splash hypo onto the print. 2. Clean negative.

UNEVEN DEVELOPMENT

Appearance: The tones are either mottled or uneven because areas are unevenly developed.

Cause: Improper immersion of print in the developer or insufficient agitation of the print may cause uneven development.

Remedy: Agitate the print properly.

UNEVEN FIXATION

Appearance: Areas of the print are darker than others. These areas are stained and are often brownish in color.

Cause: Failure to agitate prints sufficiently in hypo brings about uneven fixation.

Remedy: Use fresh hypo and agitate properly.

WHITE FINGERPRINTS

Appearance: A white fingerprint appears on the print.

Cause: The negative has been handled with hands which were wet with hypo. The hypo has dried, leaving a white fingerprint on the negative. The hypo deposit, because it is opaque, has obstructed light during exposure. As a result, the area appears white on the print.

Remedy: Cleanliness is the solution. The fingerprint often may be removed by gently rubbing the area of the negative with a soft cloth (a worn, clean handkerchief). Extreme care is necessary if hypo has been deposited on the emulsion side of the negative.

YELLOW STAINS

Appearance: Areas of the print have been stained yellow.

Cause: 1. Washing of the print may have been insufficient. 2. The print may have been examined before the hypo sufficiently fixed the image. 3. The fixing bath may have been weak. 4. The developer may have been weak, with a forced development of the print.

Remedy: Check the above causes and correct.

GLOSSARY OF TERMS

ABERRATIONS — Optical defects in a lens which cause imperfect images.

ABRASIONS — Marks on emulsion surfaces which appear as scratches, usually caused by pressure or rubbing.

ACETATE BASE — A photographic film base composed of cellulose acetate.

ACETIC ACID — The acid widely used in stop baths to stop the action of the developer before the negatives or prints are placed in the fixing bath. Also used in fixing baths.

ACID FIXING BATH — A solution of hypo to which has been added an acid (usually acetic acid) for the prupose of maintaining the hypo at the proper acidity.

AGITATION — The procedure used in processing to bring fresh solution in contact with the emulsion. This is usually done by moving the material in the solution itself, as in tray (print) development. Agitation should be consistent and is necessary for uniform results.

AIR BUBBLES — Small bubbles of air which attach themselves to the surface of an emulsion and leave a small area unaffected by the solutions. These areas appear as black spots on the print. While developing the film, sufficient agitation is necessary to prevent this from happening.

ANTI-HALATION BACKING — A coating, usually gelatin, on the back of a film, containing a dye or pigment for the purpose of absorbing light rays, thus preventing reflections from the back of the film.

APERTURE — A small opening which is usually circular. In cameras the size of the aperture is variable, regulated by an iris diaphragm. It regulates the amount of light which passes through a lens.

BLISTER — A small bubble formed between an emulsion and its base.

BLOWN-UP — Photographic slang for enlargement.

BROMIDE PAPER — A photographic printing paper in which the emulsion is made sensitive largely through silver bromide. Bromide papers are relatively fast and are usually printed by projection.

BULB	A camera exposure setting which allows the shutter to remain open as long as the shutter release is depressed.
CABLE RELEASE	A flexible shaft for operating the camera shutter to help eliminate camera movement.
CAMERA OBSCURA	A light tight box with a lens at one end and a piece of ground glass at the other. It was used by early painters as a sketching aid.
CHANGING BAG	A light-proof bag equipped with openings for the hands, in which film can be loadid or unloaded in daylight.
CHLORIDE PAPER	A photographic printing paper in which the emulsion is made sensitive largely through silver chloride. Chloride papers are usually printed by contact and require comparatively longer exposures than bromide paper.
CHLORO-BROMIDE PAPER	A photographic printing paper used basically for enlarging. Its emulsion contains a mixture of silver chloride and silver bromide.
CIRCLE OF CONFUSION	An optical term describing the size of an out of focus image point formed by a lens.
CLUMPING	The partial overlapping of grains of silver, causing an effective increase in the grain size of the emulsion.
COLOR	The sensation produced in the eye by a particular wave length or group of wave lengths of visible light.
COLOR SENSITIVITY	The response of a photographic emulsion to light of different wave lengths.
COMPLEMENTARY COLORS	Two colors of light which when combined produce white light.
CONDENSER	An optical system of lenses used in projection printing (enlargers) to collect the divergent rays of a light source and concentrate them upon the objective lens.
CONTACT PRINT	A print made by placing the emulsion side of the photographic paper in direct contact with a negative, and then passing light through the negative.
CONTRAST	The comparison of values in a negative or print. A contrasty negative or print is one in which there is a drastic difference between the whites and the blacks, with very few gray tones.

COVERING POWER   The capacity of a lens to give a sharply defined image to the edges of the film it is designed to cover at the largest possible aperture.

CUT FILM   Another name for sheet film. A flexible, transparent base coated with a light sensitized emulsion and cut into sheets of various sizes.

CYAN   A blue-green (minus red) color.

DEFINITION   The clarity of detail in the image. Also, the ability of a lens or emulsion to record fine detail. See Resolving Power.

DENSITOMETER   A device for measuring the density of a silver deposit in a photographic image. It is usually limited to measuring even densities in small areas.

DENSITY   A term used in expressing the light-stopping power of a blackened silver deposit in relation to the light incident upon it.

DEPTH OF FIELD   The distance measured between the nearest and farthest planes in the subject area which give satisfactory definition.

DEVELOPER   A solution used to make visible the latent image in an exposed emulsion. The developing agent changes exposed silver halide to black metallic silver, while leaving the unexposed halide unaffected.

DEVELOPING LATITUDE   The variation possible in the recommended developing time without noticeable difference in contrast or density.

DIAPHRAGM   The device that regulates the size of the aperture.

DIFFRACTION   An optical term used to denote the spreading of a light ray after it passes the edge of an obstacle.

DIFFUSION   The scattering of light rays from a rough surface, or the transmission of light through a translucent medium.

DIN   A European system of measuring film speed.

DISTORTION   Defects in the shape of an image caused by uncorrected lenses.

DODGING — The technique of using an opaque material to hold back light from certain areas of a print during exposure in order that the areas will be lighter.

DOUBLE EXPOSURE — The intentional or unintentional recording of two separate images on a single negative.

DOUBLE EXTENSION — The position of a camera bellows. A double extension bellows has an extended length of about twice the focal length of the lens being used.

DRY MOUNTING — A method of adhering a print to mount board by means of a thin tissue of thermoplastic material. The tissue is placed between the print and the mount, and sufficient heat applied to melt the tissue.

EASEL — A device to hold sensitized paper in a flat plane on an enlarger. It generally includes an adjustable mask to accomodate different sizes of paper.

EMULSION — The light sensitive layer, consisting of silver salts suspended in gelatin, which is spread over a permanent support such as film or paper.

EMULSION SPEED — The factor which determines the exposure necessary to produce a satisfactory image. This is commonly expressed in A.S.A., Weston or Din. numbers which have been assigned to the film. The A.S.A. number is the most commonly used.

ENLARGEMENT — A print made from a negative by projecting an enlarged image on sensitized material.

EXPOSURE — The product of time and intensity of illumination acting upon the photographic material.

EXPOSURE LATITUDE — The ability of a film or paper to allow variation in exposure without a detriment to the image quality.

EXPOSURE METER — An instrument for measuring light intensity and determining correct exposure.

F/NUMBER — A standard system for measuring the ability of a lens to gather light.

FADING — The gradual elimination, usually of the print image, due to the action of light or oxidation.

FARMER'S REDUCER	A formula, composed of potassium ferricyanide and hypo, used to reduce negative densities.
FERROTYPE PLATES (TINS)	Sheets of polished stainless steel, tin, enameled or chromium plated metal used in drying prints to obtain a high gloss finish.
FILM	A sheet or strip of celluloid coated with a light sensitive emulsion for exposure in a camera.
FILTER, LIGHT OR COLOR	A piece of colored glass or gelatin which is usually placed in front of the camera lens to compensate for the difference in color sensitivity between the film and the eye. Also used to modify or exaggerate contrast.
FILTER FACTOR	The number by which the correct exposure without the filter must be multiplied to obtain the same effective exposure with the filter.
FIXATION	The process of making soluble the undeveloped silver salts in a sensitized material by immersion in a hypo solution.
FIXED FOCUS	A term applied to a camera in which the lens is set permanently in such a position as to give a relatively sharp focus of objects from six feet to infinity.
FLAT	The expression denoting lack of contrast in a print or negative.
FOCAL LENGTH	The distance from the lens to the point where parallel light rays, as those from the sun, come into sharp focus.
FOCAL PLANE	The plane at which the image is brought to a critical focus. The position in the camera occupied by the film.
FOCAL PLANE SHUTTER	A shutter which operates immediately in front of the focal plane. It usually contains a fixed or variable sized slit in a curtain of cloth or metal which travels across the film to make the exposure.
FOCUS	A point where the light rays refracted by a lens produce a clear image.
FOG	A veil or haze over the negative or print due to undesirable light or chemical action.
FRILLING	The detachment of the emulsion from its support around the edges. It is caused by excessively heated chemicals or wash water.
GAMMA	A numerical measure of the contrast to which an emulsion is developed.

GAMMA INFINITY   The maximum contrast to which an emulsion can be developed.

GAS BUBBLES   Bubbles forcing the emulsion from the support, caused by strong chemical action, and resulting in minute holes in the negative.

GELATIN   The material used in most photographic emulsions to suspend the silver salts.

GRADATION   The range of tones in a print or negative from highlights to shadows.

GRAIN   The individual silver particles or groups of particles in the emulsion which, when enlarged, become noticeable.

HALATION   A blurred effect, resembling a halo, usually occurring around bright objects. It is caused by the reflections of rays of light from the back of the negative material.

HALF-TONES   A term used in speaking of the middle tones lying between the shadows and the highlights.

HARD   A term used to denote excessive contrast.

HARDENER   A chemical such as potassium or chrome alum which is added to the fixing bath to harden the gelatin after development.

HIGHLIGHTS   The brightest parts of the subject which are represented by the denser parts of the negative and the light gray and white tones of the print.

HYPERFOCAL DISTANCE   The distance from the lens to the nearest plane in sharp focus, when the lens is focused at infinity.

HYPO   Used in fixing solutions to make soluble the undeveloped silver salts in an emulsion and to stop the action of the developer.

INFINITY   In photography, infinity is usually considered 200-300 yards distant. Optically speaking, the light rays eminating from a subject at this distance are parallel. A distance setting on a camera focusing scale, generally beyond 50 feet.

INFRARED   Invisible rays of light inside the red end of the visible spectrum.

INTENSIFICATION   The process of building up the density of a photographic image through a chemical means.

LATENT IMAGE   The invisible image formed in an emulsion by exposure to light. It can be rendered visible by the process of development.

LENS   A lens contains one or several different shaped pieces of glass which gather the light rays reflecting from a subject and produce an image of the subject on the film plane.

LENS SHADE   A detachable camera accessory used to shield the lens from extraneous light rays.

MAGENTA   A reddish-blue (minus green) color.

MASKING   A corrective measure used in three color photography to compensate for the spectral absorbative deficiencies in pigments, dyes and emulsions. This compensation improves the accuracy of color reproduction.

MONOCHROMATIC   Pertaining to a single color.

MOTTLING   A spotty or granular appearance of either the negative or print. Uneven development is the common cause.

NEGATIVE   A photographic image on film in which the dark portions of the subject appear light and the light portions appear dark.

NITROGEN BURST   A method of agitation for developing large quantities of film (or paper in color processing). A metal or plastic distributor on the bottom of the developing tank has tiny, evenly spaced holes which release compressed nitrogen over the entire area of the tank. As the nitrogen bubbles rise to the surface, the level of the liquid rises. This rising and lowering of the developer produces the agitation. The duration and interval of the burst is timed with a timer.

OPACITY   The resistance of a material to the transmission of light.

OPAQUE   Incapable of transmitting visible light. A commercial preparation which is painted upon the negative to black out certain areas.

ORTHOCHROMATIC   A film which is not sensitive to red.
FILM

OXIDATION	The process of combining a substance with oxygen.
PANCHROMATIC FILM	A film which is sensitive to all colors.
PARALLAX	The apparent displacement of an object seen from different points of view. It is commonly encountered in photography in the difference between the image seen in the viewfinder and that which is actually recorded by the lens.
PERSPECTIVE	The illusion of three dimensions rendered on a flat surface.
pH	The acicity or alkalinity of a solution expressed in terms of the hydrogen ion concentration. A neutral solution has a pH of 7.0, an acid solution below this value, and an alkaline solution above it.
PHOTOMONTAGE	A photograph composed of several smaller photographs (a photographic collage).
PHOTOSENSITIVE	A term used to describe substances whose chemical composition may be altered by light.
PINHOLE CAMERA	A camera which has a pinhole aperture in place of a lens.
PINHOLES	Minute transparent spots in a negative which show up as black spots in a print. The most frequent cause is dust on the film.
POLA SCREEN	A screen which transmits polarized light when properly oriented with respect to the vibration plane of the incident light. When rotated to a 90° angle it will not transmit the polarized light.
POSITIVE	The print made from a negative.
PRIMARY COLOR	Any one of three components of white light: blue, green or red.
PROOF PAPER	An inexpensive paper producing a low grade or impermanent print to be viewed for making choices but not to serve as a final print. It is usually a printing-out paper (P.O.P.) which does not require a developing solution to make a visible image. The image must be observed in subdued light or it will become dark and eventually disappear.
PROPORTIONAL REDUCER	A chemical reducing solution which reduces the silver in the shadows at the same rate as it reduces that in the highlights.

RECIPROCITY LAW (FAILURE)	A law which states that the blackening of photosensitive materials is determined by the product of light intensity and time of exposure. Thus intensity is the reciprocal of time and, if one is halved, then the other must be double to obtain the same blackening.
REDEVELOPMENT	A step in the intensifying or toning procedure when a bleached photographic image is redeveloped to produce the desired results.
REDUCER	A chemical solution used to decrease the overall density of a negative.
REFLECTION	The diversion of light from any surface.
REFLECTOR	Any device used to increase the efficiency of a light source by redirecting otherwise wasted rays toward the subject to be illuminated.
REFRACTION	The bending of a light ray when passing obliquely from one medium to a medium of different density.
RESOLVING POWER	The ability of a lens to record fine detail or of an emulsion to reproduce fine detail.
RETICULATION	The formation of a wrinkled or leather-like surface on a processed emulsion due to excessive expansion or contraction of the gelatin, caused by temperature changes or chemical action.
REVERSAL	A process by which a negative image is converted to a positive. Briefly, a negative is developed, re-exposed, bleached, and redeveloped to form a positive. It is the basic principle for all color transparency processes.
REVOLVING BACK	A camera back which can be revolved so that either a vertical or horizontal picture may be obtained. Usually found in the heavier types of cameras, such as press or view cameras.
SCALE	The ratio of a linear dimension in the photograph to the corresponding dimension in the subject.
SECONDARY COLORS	Colors formed by the combination of two primary colors. Yellow, magenta, and cyan are the secondary colors.
SELF TIMER	A device on the shutter of the camera which permits the shutter to trip about ten seconds after it is released.

SEPARATION NEGATIVES	Three negatives, each of which records one of the three colors: blue, green, and red.
SEPIA TONING	A process which converts the black silver image to a brownish image. The image can vary considerably in hue, depending on the process, the tone of the original, and other factors.
SHEET FILM	A flexible transparent base coated with a light sensitized emulsion and cut into sheets of various sizes.
SHORT-STOP BATH	A solution containing an acid which neutralizes the developer remaining in the negative or print before it is transferred to the fixing bath.
SHUTTER	On a camera, a mechanical device which controls the length of time light strikes the sensitized material.
SLUDGE	A chemical precipitate or impurity which settles to the bottom of the container.
SODIUM THIOSULFATE	See Hypo.
SOFT	A term used in describing prints or negatives which have low contrast.
SPECTRUM	The colored bands of light formed by the dispersion of white light when it passes through a prism.
SPOTTING	The process of removing spots and pinholes from a negative or print.
SQUEEGEE	Either a rubber roller or strip of rubber held firmly in place for removing excess water from prints prior to drying.
STOCK SOLUTION	Photographic solution in concentrated form, intended to be diluted for use.
SUBTRACTIVE PROCESS	A process in color photography, using the colors magenta, cyan and yellow.
SUPERPROPORTION- AL REDUCER	A reducing solution which lowers the highlight density faster than it affects the shadow density.
SWINGING BACK	A camera back which can be swung through a small arc so that the divergence or convergence of parallel lines in the subject can be minimized or eliminated.

TIME-TEMPERATURE CHART	A chart indicating the developing time for a specific developer within a certain temperature range.
TONE	In photography this usually applies to the color of a photographic image or, incorrectly, to any distinguishable shade of gray.
TONING	A method for changing the color or tone of an image by chemical action.
TRANSLUCENT	A medium which passes light but diffuses it so that objects cannot be clearly distinguished.
TRANSMISSION	The ratio of the light passing through an object to the light falling upon it.
TRANSPARENCY	An image on a transparent base, which must be viewed by transmitted light. A color slide or motion picture film is an example.
TRIPOD	A three-legged support for a camera, usually with adjustments in order that the camera may be tilted, turned and the height adjusted.
TUNGSTEN	In photography, artificial illumination as contrasted to daylight. For example, film emulsion speeds are given both in tungsten and daylight.
ULTRA-VIOLET RAYS	Rays which comprise the invisible portion of the spectrum just beyond the visible violet.
VERNIER SCALE	A device used on a camera to indicate object distance.
VIEW FINDER	A viewing instrument attached to a camera, used to obtain proper composition.
VIGNETTE	Ordinarily, a dodging method used in projection printing, a process regulating the distribution of the light which reaches the print in such a way that the image obtained fades out toward the edges.
WORKING SOLUTION	A photographic solution which is ready for use.

BIBLIOGRAPHY

The following bibliography is intended only as a beginning to the vast
number of photography books. The books listed under the individual
photographer's names are the ones recently published and generally
available. A thorough bibliography may be obtained by consulting the
one-volume PHOTOGRAPHIC LITERATURE by Albert Boni (Morgan and Morgan,
New York, 1962).

HISTORY

Braine, Michel F. (Translated by David Britt)
        The Photograph: A Social History

Coke, Van Deren
        The Painter and the Photograph   1964

Doty, Robert
        "Photo-Secession", Photography as a Fine Art   1960

Gernsheim, Helmut
        Creative Photography: Aesthetic Trends   1839-1960

Gernsheim, Helmut and Alison
        A Concise History of Photography   1965
        Creative Photography, 1826 to the Present   1963
        The History of Photography (to 1941)   1955

Lacey, Peter
        The History of the Nude in Photography   1964

Lyons, Nathan
        Photographers on Photography   1966

Newhall, Beaumont
        The Daguerreotype in America   1961
        The History of Photography   1964
        Masters of Photography   1958

Pollack, Peter
        The Picture History of Photography   1958

Scharf, Aaron
        Creative Photography   1965

Taft, Robert
        Photography and the American Scene   1964

TECHNIQUE

Adams, Ansel
        Basic Photo Series (A series of five books)
                1.   Camera and Lens
                2.   The Negative
                3.   The Print
                4.   Natural Light Photography
                5.   Artificial Light Photography

Eaton, George T.
Photo Chemistry in Black and White and Color Photography   1957
Evans, Ralph M.
An Introduction to Color   1948
Eye, Film and Camera in Color Photography   1959
Lamore, Lewis
Introduction to Photographic Principles   1965
Mees, Charles Edward Kenneth
The Theory of the Photographic Process   1954
Neblette, Carroll B.
Photography, Its Materials and Processes   1962
Purves, Frederick
Focal Encyclopedia of Photography (Desk Edition)   1960
White, Minor
Zone System   1961

PHOTOGRAPHERS

Adams, Ansel
The Elequent Light   1963
This is the American Earth   1960
Atget, Eugene
The World of Atget   1964
A Vision of Paris   1963
Avedon, Richard
Nothing Personal   1964
Observations   1959
Bourke-White, Margaret
Portrait of Myself   1963
Say, Is This the U.S.A.   1941
You Have Seen Their Faces   1934
Brady, Matthew
Historian With a Camera   1955
Brandt, Bill
Perspective of Nudes   1961
Callahan, Harry
Photographs: Harry Callahan   1964
The.Multiple Image   1961
Capa, Robert
Images of War
Coburn, Alvin Langdon
A Portfolio of Sixteen Photographs   1962

144

Cartier-Bresson, Henri
        The Decisive Moment   1952
        The Photography of Cartier-Bresson   1962

Doisneau, Robert
        Paris   1956

Duncan, David Douglas
        This is War   1961
        The Private World of Pablo Picasso   1958

Evans, Frederick
        Frederick Evans   1964

Evans, Walker
        American Photographs   1962
        Let Us Now Praise Famous Men   1960

Feininger, Andreas
        The Anatomy of Nature   1956

Frank, Robert
        The Americans   1959

Gardner, Alexander
        Gardner's Photographic Sketchbook of the Civil War   1959

Heath, Dave
        A Dialogue With Solitude   1965

Kertesz, Andre
        Andre Kertesz - Photographer   1964

Klein, William
        New York
        Tokyo   1964

Lange, Dorthea
        An American Exodus   1939
        Dorthea Lange   1966

Lartique, Jacques
        The Photographs of Jacques Lartique   1963

Lyons, Nathan (with Syl Labrot, Walter Chappell)
        Under the Sun   1960

Moholy-Nagy, Laszlo
        Vision in Motion   1947

Muybridge, Eadweard
        The Human Figure in Motion   1957
        Animals in Motion   1955

O'Sullivan, Timothy H.
        Timothy O'Sullivan: America's Forgotten Photographer
        T. H. O'Sullivan: Photographer

Penn, Irving
   Moments Preserved 1960

Porter, Eliot
   The Place No One Knows 1963

Sinsabaugh, Art
   Six Mid-American Chants 1964

Siskind, Aaron
   Aaron Siskind - Photographer 1965
   Aaron Siskind - Photographs 1959

Sommer, Frederick
   1939 - 62 Photographs, An Aperture Monograph 1962

Steichen, Edward
   A Life in Photography 1963
   The Family of Man 1955

Stieglitz, Alfred
   Alfred Stieglitz: Photographer 1965
   Alfred Stieglitz, Introduction to an American Seer 1960

Strand, Paul
   Tir - A'Mhurain 1962
   Un Paese 1954
   Paul Strand Photographs 1915-1945 1945

Szarkowski, John
   The Face of Minnesota 1958

Vroman, Adam Clark
   Photographer of the Southwest 1961

Webb, Tod
   Tod Webb Photographs 1965

Weston, Brett
   Brett Weston Photographs 1966
   Photographs 1956

Weston, Edward
   The Daybooks of Edward Weston,
   Vol. I 1962
   Vol. II 1967
   Edward Weston: Photographer, An Aperture Monograph 1965

EXHIBITION PUBLICATIONS

George Eastman House
   Photography '63 / An Invitational Exhibition 1963
   Photography '64 / An Invitational Exhibition 1964
   Photography of Mid-Century 1959

Lyons, Nathan (editor)
   Photography in the Twentieth Century 1967

146

Steichen, Edward (editor)
          The Bitter Years 1935-41   1962

Szarkowski, John (editor)
          The Photographer and the American Landscape   1963
          The Photographer's Eye   1966

RELATED BOOKS

Arnheim, Rudolf
          Art and Visual Perception   1965

Bailey, Oscar and Swedlund, Charles
          Found Objects   1965

Hicks, Wilson
          Words and Pictures   1952

Kepes, Gyorgy
          Language of Vision   1951

Moholy-Nagy, Laszlo
          Vision in Motion   1956

PERIODICAL

Aperture - A Quarterly edited by Minor White

PHOTOGRAPHS:

I N D E X

150